Bigger Books, Bigger Reading Muscles

Lucy Calkins, Katie M. Wears, Rebecca Cronin, and Angela Báez

Photography by Peter Cunningham

Illustrations by Marjorie Martinelli

HEINEMANN ◆ PORTSMOUTH, NH

This book is dedicated to my coauthors, who worked with utter and absolute dedication and whose talent astonishes me.—Lucy

This book is dedicated to my mother, Katherine Hannan Wears, for unselfishly using all of your super powers to make everyone around you stronger.—Katie

This book is dedicated to Poppy, for all the lessons learned. And to Kyla, for all the lessons you will teach.—Rebecca

This book is dedicated to Mikael and Grace, my most special reading partners.—Angela

Heinemann
361 Hanover Street
Portsmouth, NH 03801–3912
www.heinemann.com

Offices and agents throughout the world

The authors and publisher wish to thank those who have generously given permission to reprint borrowed material:

From *Mouse Has Fun: Picnic*. Text copyright © 2002 by Phyllis Root. Illustrations copyright © 2002 by James Croft. Reproduced by permission of the publisher, Candlewick Press.

Pete the Cat and His Four Groovy Buttons, by Eric Litwin. Copyright © James Dean (for the character of Pete the Cat). Copyright © 2012 by James Dean and Eric Litwin. Used by permission of HarperCollins Publishers.

From *Mouse Has Fun: Pizza*. Text copyright © 2002 by Phyllis Root. Illustrations copyright © 2002 by James Croft. Reproduced by permission of the publisher, Candlewick Press.

From *Mouse Has Fun: Cat and Mouse*. Text copyright © 2002 by Phyllis Root. Illustrations copyright © 2002 by James Croft. Reproduced by permission of the publisher, Candlewick Press.

Can you see the eggs? By Jenny Giles. Copyright © 2013 HMH Supplemental Publishers. Used by permission of Cengage Australia.

"We Will Go" by Zoë Ryder White. Used by permission of the author.

Ethan and the Cat. Text copyright © 2002 by Johanna Hurwitz. Illustrations copyright © 2002 by Marilyn Hafner. Reproduced by permission of the publisher, Candlewick Press.

Wake up, Dad, by Beverly Randell. Copyright © 2013 HMH Supplemental Publishers. Used by permission of Cengage Australia.

Dragonflies © 2006 by Capstone. All rights reserved.

From *My Bug Box*, by Blanchard and Suhr. Copyright © 1999. Reprinted by permission of Richard C. Owen Publishers, Inc.

Materials by Kaeden Books and Lee & Low Books, appearing throughout the primary Reading Units of Study series, are reproduced by generous permission of the publishers. A detailed list of credits is available in the Kindergarten online resources.

Cataloging-in-Publication data is on file with the Library of Congress.

ISBN-13: 978-0-325-07701-7

Series editorial team: Anna Gratz Cockerille, Karen Kawaguchi, Tracy Wells, Felicia O'Brien, Debra Doorack, Jean Lawler, Marielle Palombo, and Sue Paro
Production: Elizabeth Valway, David Stirling, and Abigail Heim
Cover and interior designs: Jenny Jensen Greenleaf
Photography: Peter Cunningham
Illustrations: Marjorie Martinelli
Composition: Publishers' Design and Production Services, Inc.
Manufacturing: Steve Bernier

Printed in the United States of America on acid-free paper
19   VP   6

Acknowledgments

KINDERGARTEN IS A SPECIAL PLACE. This book is a tribute to kindergarten teachers everywhere who watch children transform before their eyes. You work diligently to preserve the playful, intimate nature of reading. Know that we worked with heart and soul to make sure that this unit holds true to your best beliefs about kindergarten learners and early literacy.

This unit would not have been possible without the collaboration of the community of educators who comprised by the Teachers College Reading and Writing Project—past and present. These are the people we gather with in study groups every Thursday, who answer the phone and emails at all hours when we reach out for their support, and most importantly, challenge us to outgrow ourselves. We offer a special thank you to Marjorie Martinelli for the amazing tools that she added to this book and to Amanda Hartman and Elizabeth Dunford Franco for their beautiful revisions. Thanks to Rachel Rothman and Elizabeth Moore, who provided expertise that helped us throughout the book.

This book grew out of many years of primary reading work with past staff developers whose impact is still felt. Thank you, too, to our Senior Reading Specialists, Joe Yukish and Cheryl Tyler, for your endless wisdom and input. We are also so very grateful to the members of the senior staff who co-lead the organization and inspire us with their dedication to helping schools become the best versions of themselves: Laurie Pessah, Kathleen Tolan, Mary Ehrenworth, and Amanda Hartman.

This book received thoughtful guidance from the dedicated team at Heinemann. Thanks to Abby Heim, Jean Lawler, and Felicia O'Brien for your leadership in this endeavor. Havilah Jesperson's expertise and sound reasoning throughout the editing process left an indelible mark on this book.

This version of the unit wouldn't exist without the time, help, and feedback from those who piloted it. Many thanks, especially, to the kindergarten teachers at PS 45 in Staten Island: Nicole Doria, Eileen Ward, Cheryl Bianchi, Denise Budde, Maria Squeo, Courtney McGinn, Jessica Vigliotti, Principal Christine Chavez, and Assistant Principal Nicole Gaglia. Thanks also to the kindergarten teachers at PS 452 in Manhattan: Rebecca Gartman, Shannon Reed, Brooke Josefs, Charlotte Arboleda, and Principal Scott Parker, and Assistant Principal Adam Javidi. Thanks to Paula Wilson from Arrowhead Elementary in Kenmore, Washington, and Allison Hepfer from Hamagrael Elementary in Delmar, New York. Liz Sherry supported the teachers who piloted. And a special thanks to Rebecca Rappaport Sanghvi, Allison Mihal, and Dani Sturtz; all of your time and support helped us put the finishing touches on this book. We are also grateful to Ramon Hamilton, whose careful illustrations for "We Will Go" and "My Dog" will help our kindergarten readers love the poems even more.

Finally, we would like to thank each other. The brainstorming, collaboration, and support we shared made this book better.

—Lucy, Katie, Rebecca, and Angela

Contents

BEND I   Tackling More Challenging Books

1. Tackling More Challenging Books • 2

In this session, you'll teach children that they'll need to draw on all they know (and more) to tackle the reading challenges ahead.

2. Readers Use Patterns to Help Them Read Almost Every Page • 9

In this session, you'll teach children that figuring out the pattern can help them read their books.

3. Readers Figure Out the Changing Words in the Pattern • 16

In this session, you'll teach children that they can use the picture and the first letter to solve unknown words.

4. Readers Use All of Their Super Powers to Read Pattern Breaks in Books • 22

In this session, you'll teach children to expect pattern breaks in their books and to use all of their strategies to read those parts.

5. Readers Check Their Reading • 29

In this session, you'll teach children that even after they think they have solved the words, their reading work is not finished. You will show them that readers monitor for meaning and structure, and if their reading doesn't make sense or sound right, they must fix it up.

6. Readers Use the Pattern and the Ending to Understand Their Books • 35

In this session, you'll teach children that they don't just use the pattern to help them read the words; they also use the pattern and ending to better understand their books.

BEND II   Zooming In on Letters and Sounds

7. Readers Use Their Letter-Sound Knowledge to Help Them Read the Words on the Page • 42

In this session, you'll teach children that one of their biggest sources of power is their letter-sound knowledge.

8. Readers Use Their Letter-Sound Knowledge to Help Them Read Unknown Words • 49

In this session, you'll teach children that they can use their letter-sound knowledge to solve unknown words.

BEND III Graduation: Becoming Stronger Readers

Read-Aloud and Shared Reading

 Registration instructions to access the digital resources that accompany this book may be found on p. xvi.

An Orientation to the Unit

YOU MAY NOT EVEN recognize the children in front of you because they will have changed so much over the first months of school! Children who once entered through the doorway tentatively, perhaps holding the hand of an adult, now bound right into the room, diving straight into their morning routines, all on their own. In this unit, you'll marvel—and help them marvel—at how much they've grown. You'll start with disbelief: "Wait a second, did you all get *taller*?" and lead into "Listen, readers, I'm glad you got taller and stronger and older because we have *a lot* of work to do."

Your kindergarten readers are at another important juncture. It is around this time of year when you might find yourself momentarily frozen during independent reading, as you realize, "They are reading—*conventionally*!" If you are thinking, "We did it!" or "I made it!," that's good because there is a graduation theme in this unit. Your children are moving from rereading mostly familiar texts to reading more difficult books with greater independence. In Unit 2, *Super Powers*, you probably slipped copies of "The Itsy-Bitsy Spider" into your children's book baggies after reading the song repeatedly. Now, your readers are shopping for unfamiliar books, and doing so on their own. Many have made the leap from reading level A/B books to reading books at levels C/D, and some will be beyond. This is a significant time in reading development. While children's books used to have only a few words on each page, now there may be a few lines of print on each page. While their books used to often be as simple as "I see a dog/ I see a cat/ I see a pig . . .," now their books will have far trickier patterns (or no pattern at all) and may contain dialogue, actions, prepositional phrases, high-frequency words with inflected endings, and more. In level C books, readers must use the initial consonant or consonant cluster (blend or digraph) along with meaning and syntax to read the correct word. Now, books that are approaching or at Level D are written so that readers must use meaning and syntax, and check the beginning and ending of words to read them. So both you and the children have a lot of work to do!

On the first day of the unit, you'll gather your children in close and reassure them: "As you grow bigger as readers, the books you read can get bigger and harder, too. Here's the thing: when you know *how* the books will get harder, you can use your super powers to read even those hard books."

Since children will need to carry forward the reading behaviors that they worked on in the previous unit, it makes sense to uphold the metaphor you introduced of superheroes using their reading super powers. Small groups and conferences will provide essential opportunities to introduce new texts to children and get them started reading more and more just-right books independently. Reading books for the first time, on their own, being flexibly strategic and working through difficulty, does indeed call on your youngsters to be super readers! In this unit, you will grow their bank of super power reading strategies to help them face the challenges of their new books. As the unit progresses, you'll teach readers that as their books get even bigger, their regular super powers need to get bigger, too. You'll ask readers to turn their powers up to "Extra Strength!"

This unit moves through three parts. In the first bend of the unit, you'll invite readers to study the ways books are becoming harder, so they'll be prepared for the new work they need to do as readers. You'll teach them that they can use their knowledge of how patterns go—their pattern power—to read texts with longer, more complex patterns. You'll equip them with strategies for tackling breaks in patterns, and you'll teach them to use their pattern power to think more deeply about what a book is really saying.

In the second bend of the unit, you'll rally students around the work of using their knowledge of letters and sounds—their sound power—to read tricky words. You'll teach children to first attend to the initial letter, then look to beginning consonant clusters (blends and digraphs), and finally to move their eyes to attend to the end of unknown words. By the end of this bend, your students will be using more visual information in addition to meaning and structure to solve tricky words.

The third and final bend of the unit supports students in orchestrating all the strategies they've developed to read more complex books with accuracy, fluency, and comprehension. This bend places a particular emphasis on reading high-frequency words with automaticity. You will also emphasize the importance of thinking and talking more deeply about books.

THE INTERSECTION OF READING DEVELOPMENT AND THIS UNIT

One important thing about kids at this age is that they are pattern-seekers. They do this in the world—they see patterns, join in patterns, sing patterns, clap patterns—and as you teach during this unit, you'll do the important work of taking something already important to children at this age and making it something important about reading, too.

Most of your children will enter this unit having read and reread books, songs, and poems, such as "Jack and Jill" and *Mrs. Wishy Washy*. They are already accustomed to rereading familiar texts and reading level A/B books with support (though some may have already begun moving to level C/D books and beyond). To read these level A/B texts, children have learned to rely on meaning (which includes picture support) and syntax (the song of the text) and to attend to words in sentences. And because level A/B books are designed to help readers solidify the behavior of learning to look at print, the most important visual information your readers were expected to use during the previous unit was the visual-spatial information (i.e., spaces between words).

Since level A/B books do not require readers to use sound-symbol relationships (letters and spelling patterns), they won't be reading every A/B book accurately, and that is okay. Children are not expected to read level A/B books with accuracy on their own. For example, if the picture shows two striped snakes and a child reads, "I see stripes" as "I see snakes," and does this reading work with one-to-one matching, pointing to each word as she reads along, that is just fine. Remember that you do not need to keep children reading at these levels until they do so with accuracy—once children grasp one-to-one

matching, you can graduate them to levels C/D with your support and guidance. While at those levels, they'll begin to read with more accuracy.

This means that you can move a great proportion of your students into level C/D books. In fact, we caution you against letting your students languish in level A/B books for too long. This unit supports your students in moving into level C/D books—and beyond. It is important to remember that while students can often move out of A/B books within 2–6 weeks, they often work in level C/D texts for a few months. Because the skills that are taught at levels C/D require a fair amount of teaching support, students who still need to work with A/B books will profit by participating in whole class instruction that supports the skills they'll be developing soon.

At these new levels, the pattern becomes more complicated and the endings are more complex, so readers will now need to integrate multiple sources of information as they read. That is to say, as children read, they will use phonics (visual information) as well as the pictures and the story (meaning information) to help them problem solve the text. Be sure that your children stay confident and recognize parts of reading that *do* feel familiar. Familiar people and places mean safety and security to your young students; similarly, you want to give your children the sense of "I've got this!" when they see patterns or words they know. In the long sentence that looks pretty scary, they can still find safety and security in holding on to all they've learned thus far.

In level C books, a pattern shift can happen once or several times across the book. This shift can occur within the story as well as at the end of the book. These books are more apt to tell about actions, or things that are happening. The characters *do* something. This causes changes in the sentence structure of the books. The sentences become more complex: they are longer and can include prepositional phrases.

Because of these changes in the books, it helps to channel readers not just to check the picture but also to think, "What's happening?" Throughout this unit you will help children with the important work of using meaning and thinking deeply about how a book goes. Remind readers that memorizing a language pattern might support them with *this* book on *this* day, but it isn't a strategy that can be used when reading other books. Gather children around a big book in the meeting area, and say, "Today I want to teach you that now that you are reading more challenging books, you can't just quick-check the picture to figure out the word. You have to use the *whole* picture to think about what you see and what's happening."

In this unit, you will help students integrate the sources of information and use them in combination with one another. You will coach them not only to use the picture to figure out what a word might be but *also* to use the initial consonant in the word. Some students might read a word as "puppy" by looking at the picture. At level C/D, students need to work on checking the first letter sound to make sure it is a *p* and the word begins with the /p/ sound. If the first letter is *d*, students should be prompted to crosscheck sources and fix that error. At level B, you would have accepted this type of approximation, but at level C, it's important to teach students how to self-correct these types of errors. You will also support students in attending to the beginning consonant clusters (blends and digraphs), as well as in moving their eyes across the word to make sure the word they choose matches the letters at the end, all the while remembering that they should be using meaning as their first resource. Remember that when children are reading level C/D books, they need to use visual information at the beginning and ending of words. Readers reading at these levels don't need to be prompted to attend to the internal parts of words.

While kids are reading level C/D books, it will be helpful for them to learn additional high-frequency words. Perhaps by now you'll have as many as 20 words on your word wall. Children may have their own personal copies of those words and may read through a ring of them. Students will need to continue to build up this high-frequency word bank to help them read known words with more automaticity in context. While we imagine you will support students with this throughout the day, this unit supports this work explicitly.

Fluency instruction is also built into this unit. At these levels, students are often still working to solidify their tracking. So, the first time they read a book, it will tend to be word by word. And because children will be returning to their books to read them again and again throughout each bend of the unit, you will notice that their fluency and phrasing will improve (especially when rereading). We imagine you will gather the children in close together during a minilesson and say, "Today I want to teach you that to *really* make your books come to life, you've got to be *thinking* about what's happening. On each page, you can think about what's going on and then read it in a voice that matches." You will encourage students who are reading level D books to begin to read in two-word chunks or to scoop up words using their eyes more than their fingers to track those words. Your children will be thrilled to see the dramatic leaps and bounds in how powerfully they can read their books—as will you!

It is important, too, for these readers to draw on all that they know in order to generate predictions about how the upcoming text will go. The predictions become almost a bank of possibilities for what the text might say. When a child looks at the letters, he thinks, "Which in my bank of possibilities seems closest?" Prompts can be as simple as, "What's going to be on the next page? What's going to be on the next two pages?" Then, after the child turns to actually see the words, you might say, "Were you right?" Your children, partway into a kindergarten year full of growing and exploring, are likely to be gung ho about predicting, and you can extend that enthusiasm into joy about checking their predictions, too.

In this unit, children will start using letter-sound relationships at the beginning and ending of words. As children are taking on this new work, you may need to remind them of the other things they know—meaning and syntax! Because it is easy to imagine readers reading one book after another without thinking, this unit places an emphasis on helping readers engage authentically with their texts, responding thoughtfully to them. For example, you might say, "I want to remind you that when you get to the end of your book, you don't just put the book down and start a new one! Remember, readers think about the book. Guess what else? When you *understand* the book better, you can *read* the book better. You can go back and read the book again—this time with your very best reading voice to show you understand what the book was about." And remember that one of the best ways to help readers do this is for you to think aloud about the books yourself.

You will also teach and reinforce that partners do not just read the texts but also talk about them with each other. We imagine these conversations can be just that—conversations. You can ask questions that channel readers to think inferentially as they read texts at these levels. For example, you could ask questions, such as, "How do you think the character is feeling? Why do you think she is feeling that way?" Then, too, you could ask, "Has anything like this ever happened to you?" You could also ask readers high-level judgment questions, such as, "What do you think about the illustrations in this book?" or "How do you like these characters?" That is, we don't want children to think these books are just places to practice checking some visual information (checking initial letters or beginning consonant clusters at the beginning and ending of words). Reading is not just a bunch of strategies you whip out. First and foremost, reading is thinking.

OVERVIEW

Bend I: Tackling More Challenging Books

The kindergartners in front of you have changed dramatically since day one of school. They've grown taller, lost teeth, and gained super powers that help them tackle tricky parts in their books. As you launch the unit, you'll let students know that just as they're getting bigger as people, they're also getting bigger as readers, tackling harder and harder books, and they'll need to grow bigger reading muscles to read those books. To make this challenge clear to readers, you might show them a few books, contrasting easier books with the harder books they'll be reading now, and invite them to notice all the hard things that are included in the more challenging books. Listen for students to call out their ideas, saying "There are more words!" "And more lines!" "The words are new." "And long!" These new challenges require a special new tool, and with great fanfare, you'll introduce students to a reading mat, which will help young readers to organize their reading and to read with stamina. You'll teach children that at the start of reading time, they can stack their books from easiest to hardest, using the mat, so they can work themselves up to their most challenging books. Then, you'll send students off to read, emphasizing volume of reading and transference from the previous unit of study. You'll say, "With your super powers at work, I bet you'll be able to read a ton!"

These bigger books contain new challenges, and your teaching across this bend supports students in making sense of the increasingly complex patterns in their books. The work of determining patterns and using those patterns to read on is critical for students. To kick off this work, you might first show students some simple patterns made of colored cubes, asking them to read the pattern and predict what comes next. With a few successful tries under their belts, you might say, "Wow! I can't trick you, and I don't think your books will trick you either. Figuring out the pattern helped you know what color cube was coming next. It's the same in your books. If you work hard to get the pattern, you can read *any* patterned book." This will become your students' newest super power: pattern power!

To support students in deepening their pattern power, you'll teach games such as Guess What's Next! to your children, this game will be loads of fun, with the reader reading just one page and the guesser trying to guess what the *next* page might say without reading it. The fact that the game is fun for children doesn't take away the fact that it also supports students in using their

knowledge of patterns to predict what will come next in a text. It is a good thing for children to learn to read patterned texts, expecting that some things will stay the same from one page to the next, and some things will change. You'll teach readers to think, "What will be the *same*?" and "What will *change*?" Then they can use the picture to think about what it is that will change and get their mouths ready to say the first sound of each word that is new.

Patterns are bound to break, and readers will need to use all of their super powers to read pattern breaks in books. You might say, "One reason why books become harder is because the author tricks you! Books have patterns, but then—whoops! The pattern breaks! And it usually happens on the last page." Sure, these surprise endings are fun for readers, but they also take hard work to read, so you'll say to readers, "We might need to bring two, or three, or even *every* power to this job!"

As kindergartners move into harder and harder texts, it becomes increasingly important for them to monitor for meaning and for structure, so they can be ready to fix up their reading when it doesn't make sense or sound right. You'll teach students to be careful readers, tackling problems head on. "Just like we don't walk right past problems in our classroom, we don't read right past problems in our reading," you might say. You will teach students that readers stop and ask, "Did that make sense? Did that sound right?" and if not, they try to fix it up. Expect to hear a chorus of "Oopses!" coming from your students, and you'll celebrate that students are checking themselves, saying, "Oops!" whenever something is not quite right.

Patterns are certainly useful for helping students read the words in their books smoothly, but by the end of the bend, you'll extend this work and teach children that patterns can also help them to better understand their books. You might say, "When you get to the end of a book, you can think about how the whole pattern goes and what part of the pattern changes at the end. Then, you ask yourself, 'What is this whole book really saying?'" You might demonstrate using *It's Super Mouse*, thinking first about the pattern and saying, "Oh, he's jumping off so many things. On *every* page he jumps off something. The things on every page get higher and higher!" Then, zoom in on the pattern break. "Maybe that's why he falls at the end—he tries to jump off something that is way too high! Mouse wants to be Super Mouse and fly, but he crashes to the ground instead. Were you thinking that, too?" In this way, you'll support students in using their pattern power to read more smoothly and to think about the entire book.

Across the bend, we suggest you make use of various balanced literacy components to support readers in strengthening their pattern power while also drawing on all the powers they developed in the previous unit. During a share session, for example, you could gather students together to write a pattern book using interactive writing, saying, "I thought, maybe, we could work together to write a new book—and maybe we could make it our very own pattern book! Let's make this be a book about kids who like to read and let's make *you* be the stars of this book." While your focus on that day would be on using the pattern to predict what happens next, another day's share might use shared writing to write pattern breaks for the ending of the book.

Bend II: Zooming In on Letters and Sounds

In the second bend, your teaching will focus on increasing student's understanding of sound-symbol relationships, or "sound power" as the kids will call it. As readers move into level C books, sound power becomes a defining behavior. As we mentioned earlier, a child reading level A/B books is doing the work you expect her to do correctly if she uses a miscue that still makes sense (M) and sounds right (S). If a child read, "I see a bunny," when the text said, "I see a rabbit," your response might have been "You are right, it could say *bunny*! That makes sense, doesn't it?" You may have added, "It could also say *rabbit*, right? That would make sense too." Now, however, as your kindergartners move into level C texts, your expectations will shift, and it will become essential for children to also check the first letters in a word. If the reader reads *bunny* when the word is *rabbit*, you'll want to teach the reader to check that answer and to self-correct. You'll probably say, "Does that make sense? Sound right?" and after the child says yes to those questions, you'll ask "Does it look right?" You might point to the letters in the word (V), saying, "Hmm, something doesn't look quite right." That is, in books at level C and beyond, readers are expected to integrate information from the picture and the initial consonant sound to determine what the tricky word is saying. This bend supports students in strengthening their sound power, helping them first use the initial letter, then beginning consonant clusters (blends and digraphs), and then ending sounds to read tricky words.

You'll begin this bend with an out-of-the-ordinary day, launching students into a study of alphabet books designed to flex their letter-sound muscles. You'll build excitement and express purpose for the study, perhaps declaring,

"Readers, we are definitely learning more about letters and sounds. Alphabet books help us do that. Some people call these Alphabet Power Stations because readers can go to them to get more letter and sound power. But to get that power, you don't just read, read, read these books. Instead you use the book to help you think about letters and sounds."

You'll present these alphabet books like a miraculous gift, and go on to say, "Just like always, I'm going to look carefully at the pictures in my book to figure out how it works. In this book, each page shows a letter and a few pictures of different animals (to give an example) whose names begin with that letter. Watch how I use the letters and the sounds to help me figure out what is on each page." You might pause at a picture of a monkey on the *A* page in a book, try the sound a few ways, and discover that *A* is for *ape*. Then, you'll send students off to stations around the room, alphabet books in hand, to make choices about the work they do with a partner. Some partners might linger on one page in the alphabet book, trying to add more words. Others might sing their way through the alphabet song on each new page, stopping when they get to the letter featured on a page. Still some might play "Same and Different," laying two alphabet books next to each other and noting their similarities and differences.

As the bend continues, you'll teach students to extend their knowledge of letters and sounds to read unknown words. To do this requires close and careful looking, so you might invite readers to pull out pretend magnifying glasses, saying, "Let's zoooooom into this word. Get your special magnifying glasses ready to look really, really closely at the letter at the beginning." Then you might uncover a hidden word, prompting the children to use both picture and sound power to figure out the tricky word.

Many of the words students read will include blends, and you'll want to teach them to be on the lookout for blends in their books. You might say, "Readers and writers don't just blend colors and chocolate milk. They also blend sounds." To get partners practicing reading words with blends, you'll introduce a game called "Alphabet Pop It!" that students can play during partner reading. "Here's how you play. You point to something in the picture, and then you let the first sound that word makes *pop* right out of your mouth. Then, you can think about what letter or letters make that sound and say those letters." This helps ensure students are warmed up if they encounter those words on the page.

Soon, you'll extend this work, teaching students that after they look at the beginning of words, they can move their eyes toward the endings to make sure they're reading the correct word. To demonstrate the importance of reading word endings correctly, you might pull out a picture of a sign reading "Fresh Donuts" and tell students how when you were on your way to work that morning, you saw this sign that said "Free Donuts," so you parked your car and ran like crazy to the counter shouting, "I want free donuts!" Explain how you quickly realized that you'd read only the first part of the word, saying, "I was reading the word so quickly that I didn't look all the way to the end of the word! If I just looked a little bit further, I would have realized it had /sh/ at the end: 'Fresh Donuts'" You'll coach students as they use beginning and ending letters to read unknown words.

Later, you might put on your best game announcer voice and loudly say, "Ladies and gentlemen, get ready to play 'Guess the Covered Word!'" That exercise supports students in orchestrating different cueing systems when reading a word. "When you get to a covered word, you will get your mouth ready with the first sound and think, 'What would make sense and sound right in the sentence?' Then, you will make some guesses and I will write them down. Afterward, we will uncover the rest of the word so you can look all the way to the *end* of the word and check your guesses." Use a large, shared text to practice this work, covering several words you and your students can work through. Before, students checked their reading, asking, "Does it make sense? Does it sound right?" Now, they will ask a new question: "Does it look right?"

This focus on word solving tricky words can lead to students slowing down to solve each word they come to, so you'll want to teach them that readers use different strategies on different words. You might say, "When reading *some* words (words that aren't snap words), readers bring out their magnifying glasses and look closely at the letters. But when they come to a snap word, they put the magnifying glass away! They don't need to slow down or read closely. They just look at the word and know it in a snap."

As the bend draws to a close, you'll gather readers to celebrate their newly strengthened sound power and sing a sound power song: "We have sound power/Yes we do/We have sound power/How 'bout you?"

Bend III: Graduation: Becoming Stronger Readers

In the third bend, you'll call your readers *graduates*, turn on a graduation song, and parade around the room. As students make their way to the meeting area,

you'll harken back to the beginning of the unit, saying, "You are different readers now than you were when we started our unit. You've grown so strong as readers that *now* you are ready to graduate. You are graduating to more challenging books. Your books are changing—and *you* have to change, too. Your powers need to graduate, they need to be able to do new things." Your big work across this bend will be to support students in adjusting, in turning up their reading strategies, as they move up levels of text, and you'll support them in building on their reading super powers to tackle new challenges.

With their extra-strength picture power in hand, you'll teach students that it's no longer enough to look at a picture and let it just help with figuring out one word. You'll teach readers they can study the pictures and say all that is happening in the picture and then use that information to read longer, more complex patterns. As your readers study pictures and begin to notice not just what is in the picture but also where it is, they may need support differentiating between prepositions. For the share one day, you might gather students together to play "Simon Says," focusing on words that describe *where* something is. You might say, "Lift your leg and clap your hands *under* your knee."

As books become more complex, they can be less heavily patterned, and readers will need to do more work to figure out what each page says. You might let students in on this change, saying, "As you get older, the patterns that helped you read might fall away, just like the training wheels will eventually come off your bikes. And you're going to need stronger powers to read those new books." When this happens, you'll coach students to use their snap word power and their extra-strength picture power to figure out the tricky parts. You'll let students know that as they get older and read more, they'll know more and more snap words. "The words you see over and over eventually become snap words. Reading and rereading pattern books has turned your brains into snap word machines!"

Your readers will need to recognize and read high-frequency words no matter what, even when they include endings, so you will want to teach readers to read on the lookout for these words. This is tricky work. You might tell the story of seeing a friend in a hat and not recognizing her at first, and then connect this to snap words, saying, "Sometimes familiar words hide. When a word looks like a stranger to you—look again. Ask yourself, 'Does this look like another word I know?' Chances are that it could be a familiar snap word with a new ending." Some examples that your readers might encounter when reading level C/D book include words such as *plays*, *looking*, *comes*, and *jumped*.

Of course, it's not enough for students to just read books smoothly and read words without stopping to think, so you'll want to support them in deepening their comprehension of texts and their talk. Many of your children will be reading stories, and before the bend draws to a close, you'll want to teach them to use their knowledge of how stories go to think about the story and predict what might happen next. You will also teach students that the way they think and talk about books needs to grow and change. You might say, "You are ready to bring extra strength to your book talk power," and then you might teach students to think more about the characters, what they are doing, their feelings, and why they feel that way.

We suggest you conclude the unit by leading your class in a celebration of all the work they have done to become stronger readers. Celebrate with a graduation ceremony, cheering on kids and reminding them of their new powers that will allow them to read so many books. You might send them off by adapting a line from *Oh, the Places You'll Go*, saying, "Readers, today is your day! Your books are waiting. So, get on your way!"

ASSESSMENT

Take and study running records.

As the unit progresses, continue to use running records to plan for instruction. Keep a close eye on the reading behaviors students have mastered and the behaviors they still need to practice. For example, if a student is new to reading level C books and already uses the picture to make guesses and substitutions but is not crosschecking with the first letter, coach her to check the first letter after checking the picture each time.

Once your readers have been working with level C/D books for a month or two, you'll need to think about when to move them to level E/F/G books. The general rule of thumb is that when a child has read an assessment text with 95% or 96% accuracy and strong comprehension, you move him up a level. But you'll probably check the child's accuracy and comprehension on *any* book in his book baggie.

Analyze other assessments to get a comprehensive view of your readers.

Because of the important role high-frequency words play in beginning reading, you will want do an assessment of children's current high-frequency words at the start of this unit. You can glean information by asking children to read through high-frequency word lists, and use that as well as running records and writing samples to plan for high-frequency word instruction.

For children who aren't yet reading conventionally or demonstrating letter-sound correspondence when writing, you will want to assess their phonological awareness. Check to see if these students can show you that they hear sounds in a word. Can they take a word—*pig*, for example—and say it slowly, isolating the component sounds (/p/ /i/ /g/)?

As you watch for signs of growth but don't always see a steady line of forward progress, take heart! Anyone who knows anything about development in these early stages will tell you that progress is two steps forward, one step back. Learning involves approximation, error, and resilience, as well as many opportunities to try again. As children move from "starting to" to "doing with independence," you will be there to both scaffold and to plan for the release of that scaffold. Leverage read-aloud, shared reading, guided reading, and word study to offer the multiple encounters with the reading work that your students need. Remember also that you may want to repeat any of the minilessons in this book, perhaps with a different demonstration text. Or you might choose to duplicate a portion of a session, such as a share or the mid-workshop teaching. You'll always be responding to your children, pinpointing strengths and personal next steps—a pedagogy that does not live inside any one unit.

Although, yes, we encourage you to revisit lessons and linger, we also want to say, "Don't dally too long!" You'll want time for other units. You most certainly won't wait until every child is in control of every strategy to move forward in this unit. Instead, plan to use conferring and small-group work to support readers who need that help.

Use your assessment data to plan curriculum.

At the end of the unit, you might find that your students could benefit from repeated practice with some of the work in this unit. If that is the case, you might refer to the unit titled "Readers Are Resourceful: Tackling Hard Words and Tricky Parts in Books" in *If . . . Then . . . Curriculum: Assessment-Based Instruction, Grades K–2*. In that unit, you'll find that many of the same skills and strategies are taught with a different spin, allowing you to give your kids some extra practice.

A different option might be to teach the unit titled "Growing Expertise in Little Books: Nonfiction Reading" (from the same book) before moving on to

Unit 4, *Becoming Avid Readers*. The word work you introduce in this unit will apply perfectly to the work children will do in nonfiction books. Keep in mind that your students will have a chance to read nonfiction in Unit 4 as well.

In any case, the information you've collected in this unit (from running records, conferring notes, and other assessments) will help you track students' progress not just in this unit, but across units.

GETTING READY

Gather enough just-right books for each reader to sustain independent and partner reading.

Children will shop for books in the classroom library each week to replenish their personal supply of books. You might create and introduce a book shopping schedule with a bit of fanfare—yet another sign that the children are growing into bigger, stronger, and more responsible readers.

Keep in mind that level A/B/C books typically only take a minute or so to read, so your children will need many books in their book baggies to keep them engaged during reading time. Supplying each child with ten to twelve books at these levels each week is usually sufficient and will still involve a whole lot of rereading during the week. At this point of the year, you'll need a very large number of books at levels B, C, and D (and above), so that children can shop for enough books to last them for the week and get new books the next week. If you have twenty-four kids and each one needs ten B/C/D books, that's 240 books each week! Some schools have an abundance of books, so this is doable. If you don't have enough books at these levels, however, you might consider the following recommendations:

- Look at your guided reading inventory. Many teachers have a surplus of guided reading text sets for levels A–F. If this is the case, after you have led a guided reading group on a book, disperse those books into the group member's baggies. Round them back up for a later guided reading group followed by circulation.

- Group the books you *do* have into several A/B, C/D, or E/F baskets and then put these baskets on tables. During private and partner reading time, the readers reading these levels may not be able to read from

personal book baggies but may, instead, sit at the tables and read a book from the basket. Then, they put it back and choose another.

Both the contents of their book baggies and the ways in which children shop for books will depend on their just-right, or independent, reading level. Here is a guideline for each week:

- Children who are emergent readers (still developing one-to-one correspondence) can shop for ten to twelve A/B books and an emergent storybook, in addition to many shared writing texts you've made together, and familiar songs and poems.

- Children reading books at levels A/B conventionally (with one-to-one correspondence) will shop for six to ten A/B books and a few level C books.

- Children reading books at level C and on conventionally will shop for ten to twelve just-right books, and possibly a few at the next level.

- All children can have a collection of personal copies of familiar shared reading texts that you will add to each week. Many teachers store these in a small binder, notebook, or folder that can fit into children's book baggies.

Organize your books in a way that makes it easy for children to find their just-right books, boosting agency and independence.

Because there is a range of difficulty within most any text level, you might consider organizing your books in different baskets with the progression of difficulty in mind, to help children find their just-right books more efficiently. For example, you might comb through your baskets that contain level C books, and reorganize them so that one basket holds books that are more highly patterned (and usually easier), and another has books that have a story structure (usually more difficult). Find a visual way to direct children to the basket that best matches them as readers, such as a label or a different colored tub.

You will want to orient children to what their just-right books look like. This can usually best be accomplished in a one-on-one conversation, and possibly with a "shopping list" slipped into the book baggie as a reminder. That is to say, you can privately tell children the level of text that they can currently read independently, with the express purpose of helping them locate books that will make them feel strong as readers. Books are leveled to help readers find them, but avoid identifying children as levels. There is no need to post levels publically for the children to "use;" plus they will be growing so quickly that their just-right book basket will be ever-changing!

Plan to support children with book introductions during conferring time or as they shop for books.

If you teach this unit during January or February of kindergarten, the benchmark for this time of year is B/C with a book introduction, although if you have taught the previous units, we find most children will be reading at level C. Early in the week, you'll want to make it a practice during reading time to quickly meet with children who are reading texts at levels A–C and introduce their books. These readers are working on carrying the pattern across the pages, and you can help by supporting meaning and establishing that pattern in your book introduction. As you watch these readers shop for books, you may notice that they feel unsure. Likely, all that they need is the title, gist, and pattern unlocked for them! Also, along with a place to jot conferring notes, you might prepare an extra stack of books to introduce and give to readers on days when all of the books in their baggies are ones they have read twenty times already.

The important thing is that *you* need to feel absolutely 100% confident about giving book introductions so you don't resist doing them because you feel unprepared. The books your children will be reading are brief enough that you can read the book and prepare for the introduction in a minute. You might give them the title and read the first page or two so that they can learn the pattern of the book and understand what is happening inside. And as you watch more children working with the same book, you become more proficient at introducing that book!

Collect texts you will use for minilessons, as well as for guided reading and other types of small groups.

You should, of course, make choices about books to use as minilesson demonstration texts in this unit. Or, if you prefer, use the ones we demonstrate with, also available in the trade pack:

- *Mouse Has Fun* by Phyllis Root
- *Can you see the eggs?* by Jenny Giles
- *Wake Up, Dad!* by Beverley Randell

Other books that we reference are interchangeable with similar texts or are excerpts included in the sessions:

- *Pete the Cat and His Four Groovy Buttons* by Eric Litwin
- *Oh, the Places You'll Go!* by Dr. Seuss
- *Ethan's Cat* by Joanna Hurwitz

For guided reading and small-group shared reading, you'll need to gather multiple copies of unfamiliar texts at instructional levels and be ready to give these books to your readers to reread for some time after each one of your lessons. These essential sessions will allow you to support your children's developing reading processes, closely monitor their growth, and expand the number of books they have access to daily. You might also create a weekly or monthly schedule to help you plan your sessions and the frequency of your meeting with each group.

Teach high-frequency words and add them to the word wall on a regular basis.

It is helpful if part of your kindergarten word study curriculum supports children building a set of known high-frequency words. At the start of this year, you probably began with a name study. The students' names will be the first words on your word wall. After the name study, we imagine you began to introduce your class to high-frequency words. By the time you start this unit, you'll likely have a handful of words on the word wall. You might have introduced your class to approximately twelve to fifteen high-frequency words before you begin this unit. By January of kindergarten, most teachers plan to introduce one to three high-frequency words a week.

It is important to plan for high-frequency word instruction in both isolation and in context. When working with high-frequency words, you will want to think about the three ways of remembering. You will want the children to see the word, say the word and spell it, and move the word (writing the word in the air, on a partner's back, or on a dry erase board). You will want to have lots of opportunities for children to practice reading and writing high-frequency words. To help with this, we recommend introducing word rings to your children. A word ring is a tool that we refer to in Bend II of this unit. A word ring can act as a personal word wall; you can write each word wall word that you've studied on a small card and attach the cards to a book ring or other holder so that the children can flip through and read the familiar words as a warm up for reading. You can also have differentiated word rings, where each reader's ring contains the words she or he is working on reading in context. For other high-frequency word activities, you can refer to the guide book, *A Guide to the Reading Workshop, Primary Grades*, Chapter 11.

You will want to make sure that you introduce high-frequency words commonly found in level C books and beyond. High-frequency words found in level C books could include words such as *like, look, said, come, play, did, for, get, have, here, him, of, she, will,* and *you*. High-frequency words often found in level D books are *all, down, saw, that, they, this, was, went, what, where, when,* and *with*. You might also look through your own leveled baskets, noticing other high-frequency words that occur frequently.

Plan ahead for the tools you will need to prepare and distribute.

- Prepare a reading mat for each child (see Session 1 and online resources).
- Create word rings for each reader that contain differentiated sight words based on your assessments.
- Have the extra-strength icons ready to add to the "We Are Super Readers!" chart.
- Make copies of the individual super powers charts, one for each student.

READ-ALOUD AND SHARED READING

Collect the texts you want to read aloud to your students during this unit.

You will want to read aloud and talk about books with your children every day. The read-aloud plan for *Dragonflies* by Margaret Hall is replicable and can be adapted to other daily read-alouds in this unit. This book was chosen because so many kindergarten children are fascinated by bugs, animals, and the world around them, and the photographs in the book are large, vibrant, and engaging.

You will also want to choose some read-alouds that will rally kids around the themes of the bends. In Bend I you will do lots of teaching around pattern books. *Pete the Cat and His Four Groovy Buttons* by Eric Litwin is a book that we refer to in minilessons in the first bend. We selected it because it is a beloved pattern book that many classrooms and school libraries already own, and also because it is a story of resilience, of bouncing back when things are hard or disappointing. This is a mindset we hope for all readers to develop in this unit and always! If you do not have access to this book, HarperCollins also offers it as a free downloadable audiobook, and you can find the link in the online resources.

For the beginning of Bend II, you'll need to gather various alphabet books to read aloud and for partnerships to read. These alphabet books should illustrate letter-sound correspondence, like *A is for Angry* by Sandra Boynton. Some other favorites are *Dr. Seuss's ABCs, ABC Kids* by Laura Ellen Williams, *Eating the Alphabet* by Lois Ehlert, *Miss Spider's ABCs* by David Kirk, and *The Jazzy Alphabet* by Sherry Shahan. Keep in mind that alphabet books range in topic and difficulty from quite simple to highly complex, so keep an eye out for books that will appeal to particular readers in your class.

In Bend III, we use an excerpt from *Oh, the Places You'll Go!* by Dr. Seuss to carry on a theme of graduation. You might decide to read aloud the whole book during read-aloud time. Other books that would add to the excitement of Bend III include *Curious George Curious You: On Your Way!* by H. A. Rey, *I Knew You Could!: A Book for All the Stops in Your Life* by Craig Dorfman, and *Yay, You! Moving Out, Moving Up, Moving On* by Sandra Boynton. None of these, however, is essential, and you can substitute your own favorites.

Gather the texts you plan to use during shared reading each week.

The shared reading text referenced during this unit is *My Bug Box* by Pat Blanchard and Joanne Suhr, and it is a level E book. The book is available in the trade pack but can also be purchased as a big book from Richard C. Owen Publishers. We chose *My Bug Box* because it is an engaging story with some repetition that readers can lean on when reading in unison. It also offers opportunities for children to encounter prepositional phrases, contractions, inflected endings, and more complex pictures—all common characteristics of books at level C and beyond. The five-day plan using *My Bug Box* can be found in the shared reading section of this book, and coaches children to draw on a repertoire of strategies for solving unfamiliar words, particularly searching for meaning by using the picture and looking at initial sounds to crosscheck visual information, which is one of the big goals for your children during this unit. You can also use this section as a template to help you plan for other shared reading sessions using different books.

Since shared reading sessions can incorporate more than one text, "Hickory Dickory Dock" was chosen as the warm-up song. You will also want to choose other songs, poems, chants, and nursery rhymes that can become your warm-up texts for shared reading in the weeks that follow, because they can support many kindergarten word study concepts (early literacy concepts, phonological awareness, letter knowledge, letter-sound relationships) and become familiar material for readers to read during reading workshop. Remember that the poems and songs introduced in this unit can also become warm ups. These texts often become class favorites, with children begging to read them again and again!

❧ ONLINE DIGITAL RESOURCES

A variety of resources to accompany this and the other Kindergarten Units of Study for Teaching Reading are available in the Online Resources, including charts and examples of student work shown throughout *Bigger Books, Bigger Reading Muscles*, as well as links to other electronic resources. Offering daily support for your teaching, these materials will help you provide a structured learning environment that fosters independence and self-direction.

To access and download all the digital resources for the Kindergarten Units of Study for Teaching Reading:

1. Go to **www.heinemann.com** and click the link in the upper right to log in. (If you do not have an account yet, you will need to create one.)
2. **Enter the following registration code** in the box to register your product: RUOS_GrK
3. Under **My Online Resources**, click the link for the ***Kindergarten Reading Units of Study***.
4. The digital resources are available under the headings; click a file name to download.

(You may keep copies of these resources on up to six of your own computers or devices. By downloading the files you acknowledge that they are for your individual or classroom use and that neither the resources nor the product code will be distributed or shared.)

Tackling More Challenging Books

IN THIS SESSION, you'll teach children that they'll need to draw on all they know (and more) to tackle the reading challenges ahead.

CONNECTION

GETTING READY

✓ Write, "Challenging books have . . ." across the top of a blank piece of chart paper to record children's observations during the minilesson. This chart will only be used for today's minilesson (see Teaching and Active Engagement).

✓ Display the chart "We Are Super Readers!" from the previous unit (see Teaching, Active Engagement, and Mid-Workshop Teaching).

✓ Choose a demonstration text that has one word and picture per page, a second that has a few sentences per page, and a third book that is at level C with a pattern that changes at the end, to show how some books are harder than others (see Teaching and Active Engagement).

✓ Prepare reading mats for each student, using letter-size manila file folders. Inside, put a green dot on the left (where students will place books to be read) and a red dot on the right (for books once they have been read). Students will use these for the remainder of the year. Templates for the reading mats are available in the online resources (see Link).

✓ Display the Private Reading/Partner Reading sign from Unit 2, *Super Powers.* Be ready to display this every day (see Link).

✓ Choose a level B or C text to share with the kids either by using a big book version or by displaying it under the document camera. Select a text with a repeating pattern (see Share).

Celebrate your childrens' signs of growth—lost teeth and new inches—and use this to suggest they are ready to grow as readers as well.

I sang the gathering song, and the children joined in as they came to the meeting area, taking their seats beside their reading partners.

> We are gathering.
> We are gathering
> On the rug,
> On the rug.
> Everyone is here now,
> finding their own space now.
> We are here.
> We are here.

"Oh my goodness. I see some kids who lost a tooth over the holidays! Holy moly. How many of you lost a tooth?" Hands shot up. "That's amazing. We were just out of school for two weeks, and so many things changed in that time.

"And wait a second, did you get *taller?* Ben, will you stand up so we can see how tall you have become?" He scrambled to his feet. "Wait! I'm seeing other kids who got taller, too! Will *all* of you stand up?"

The kids clambered to their feet. "What did you eat over vacation? I'm seeing such long legs. And I swear your hair even got longer.

"Listen, readers, I'm glad you got taller and stronger and older, and I am hoping your brains grew too because it is a new year, and we have *a lot of work* to do."

❖ **Name the teaching point.**

"Today I want to teach you that as you grow bigger as readers, the books you read can get bigger and harder too. Here's the thing: when you know *how* the books will get harder, you can use your super powers to read *even* those hard books."

TEACHING AND ACTIVE ENGAGEMENT

Suggest that when kids know how books get harder, they can get themselves ready to tackle those new challenges.

"Today I want to show you how books go from easier to harder, and then we can talk about how you can get even more power to read these harder and harder books. This is going to be grown-up work, so I am glad you grew so much.

"I'm going to show you a bunch of books, and will you all help me *study* these books like you studied leaves during our writing workshop unit when you became scientists? Will you help me notice the way books go from easier to harder and to *hardest*? We will put the books into piles: easy, hard, hardest."

I placed the first book under the document camera for students to begin studying. We looked at the first two pages. "Here is one book. What do you think? Easy or hard?" I gave the children time to think. "Easy. Sure. Why? Because there is only one picture and one word on each page."

Then I showed them a book that had a few sentences on each page and said, "Now look at this book. You and your partner can study the first couple of pages of this book and decide, 'Is it easier? Or is it harder than this one?' Ready?" I reminded students to look closely at the pictures and the words and to use some of their super powers to help them as they talked to one another.

"Yes, you are talking about what makes some of this book harder. And the really cool thing is that I already see you calling up even more super powers so that you are able to read these hard parts.

"So, which one is harder?" All the students pointed to one of the books, and I asked, "Why? What makes it harder? Turn and tell your partner all the things that you think make it harder."

This lead assumes that you are teaching the unit right after the winter holidays, when kids have been away for a stretch of time. If you teach the unit at another time, you can mention that recently you looked back at pictures from the start of the year and you realized that since those first days of school, they've grown before your eyes.

Notice that here we build a buzz around moving to harder books, even though not every child will be moving to new levels right now. The reality is that children will encounter some challenge in any just-right book. The opportunity to face difficulty and work productively to conquer it is what promotes growth!

On chart paper, make a list of the characteristics of harder books, gathering children's input.

I listened in and reconvened the children. "Let's list some of the hard things that you've noticed."

Thumbs shot up, and soon I was restating and recording kids' comments. "So you are saying that for starters, the easier book has fewer words on a page—maybe just a word, like this book," and I pointed to the first book we looked at, "and the harder book has *more* words?" I jotted that down. "What else?" Soon we'd made this list:

This charted list will only be used in today's minilesson. Your list doesn't need to follow this order. While you will want to honor and record your students' observations, you can also gently guide the discussion by saying, "Did anyone notice . . ." and in that way, get certain items added to the list.

> Challenging books have . . .
> - more words, more lines
> - new words
> - longer words

"Look, here's another one. Let's look at this book all the way through and think, Is it easier than these? Harder? And why? Ready?" I placed a level C book under the document camera and listened to partnerships read and talk about the pages. As I turned the pages toward the end of the book, most of the kids were reading in unison. Then we got to the last page. "Uh-oh! This seems hard! It looks different from the other pages."

We read the last page together and I said, "What do you think? Easier? Harder?"

"Medium!" Ben shouted out.

"Medium, like, in between these two. What made this one hard?" The students agreed that the last page was harder than the rest. I then added a bullet to our chart and said, "That ending really was a surprise! *And* it was harder to read! I'm going to write, 'surprise endings.' That can make a book hard!"

> - surprise endings

"Whoa, readers, you noticed lots of things about these books that were easier and harder! Knowing the things that might be hard can help you!"

LINK

Recap today's teaching and remind students that they are going to find, and learn about, new sources of power to help them read new books.

"In this new unit, you'll learn new powers to tackle these hard parts in books. But don't forget, you already know so much! Let's read the chart listing the super powers, to remind you of what you already know and can use!" I raised my pointer to the first word, and we read the chart out loud together.

"Today, you are going to be reading the *new* books that you picked from the library. Every day, before you read, you can quickly sort your books from easier to harder. This way, you can get your super powers warmed up and you will be ready to tackle the harder books!

"To help you organize your reading, I'm giving you a new tool. It's a *reading mat!*

"On the side with the green dot, you can stack your books to read. Put the easy books on the top and the harder and harder books lower down." I showed the children what I meant. "Then read the first easy book. When you're done, put it over on the side of your mat with the red dot." I demonstrated moving a book and placing it cover down. "Then read the next book, and move it over too.

"When you have finished reading all your books and have them on the red dot side, you can read your way back! You'll find out just how much you can read today! With your super powers at work, I bet you'll be able to read a *ton!*" Putting up the Private Reading sign, I sent everyone off to read.

Stacking books on the reading mat allows kids to plan for and be intentional about their reading. Most readers will approximate stacking books from easier to harder and some will come up with their own ways to stack. This is something to celebrate!

FIG. 1–1 Reading mat stacked with books ready to read

Create a Buzz around the New Unit

AT THE START OF ANY NEW UNIT, you'll want to get a buzz going around the work of that unit. That will be tricky to do in this unit because the fact that you have announced that kids will be *ready* to read harder books doesn't actually make that *true*! You are essentially getting kids to role-play their way into the identity of a confident reader, able to say, "I'm someone who can read harder and harder books."

The easiest way to make this statement a true one is to dramatically increase the number of quick book introductions you do. Many of your readers will only be able to read harder books—and presumably for many children this will mean level C books—if they have the scaffolding of a book introduction. If you have multiple copies of

level B/C/D books, that'll put you in especially good stead because you can do book introductions with groups of children. If not, then you'll introduce books to individual readers.

You might pull a small group together and say, "Readers, come close. I want to tell you about this *really cool* book that I have for you. It's a *challenging* book. Are you ready to get your reading muscles strong, so you can tackle it? You are? Super! Let me tell you a bit about this book."

Then read the title and, in a sentence, tell the children what the book is about. You'll want to turn to the first page and read it aloud showing the picture and pointing under the words as you read them. Then you might invite the children to read the page with you before proceeding to another page. You'll want to be mindful of new vocabulary or tricky language structures and use these in your introduction. You could point to the picture of a new thing and talk about it. Asking children to join you in saying something about it would encourage them to use the word. Children can also find the word in the text. After you introduce the book, give a copy to each child who received the book introduction and send them back to their reading spots, adding these new texts to their book baggies.

During conferences, you can also give readers support with new books, saying, "Remember, when you are getting ready to read a new book, it helps to look the book over and think what it'll be about. Will you do that now, while I watch?" You'll want to get the child to think aloud so you can chime in to support her work. If the book is titled "We Go!" and the first page shows a beach, and the reader says, "A beach," you might nod and help her with the language of the text by saying, "So let's remember the title. 'We Go!' Do you think this page might say, 'We go to . . . ,'" and the child will add, "the beach." You might then ask her to go back and reread the whole page with one-to-one matching. Be sure you then pull back in your level of involvement, saying almost nothing as you let the reader progress to the next pages. Prepare to live with the child making a few miscues—a good trade-off for independence.

MID-WORKSHOP TEACHING
Readers Use the Strategies They Know

Standing in the middle of the room, I said, "Readers, I know we had a *long* vacation from school. But don't let that *long* time away make you forget the super stuff you already know how to do." I stood next to the "We Are Super Readers" chart and pointed to the first line. "How many of you are remembering to use your pointer power, giving every word one tap, even the longer words?" I made a power gesture, fist raised, and children adopted the gesture to show that absolutely, they used pointer power. "Super! And how many of you are remembering to use picture power when you're stuck on a word?" Again, fists were raised. "And how many of you are remembering to use sound power and check that the first letter matches the word you are reading?" The children shot their fists into the air.

"Your Super Readers chart can remind you of *all* the super reading powers you already have!"

TRANSITION TO PARTNER TIME
Partners Read Books from Easiest to Hardest

I flipped our sign over to the partner side and got the children's attention. "Readers, you remember how to read with partners, right? Show me how you will sit to read with partners." The children all reconfigured themselves so they were sitting hip to hip. "Show me how you'll hold a book to read," I said, and partners held one book between them.

"Partners, you'll notice things are a little different now because you each have a reading mat. What will you do with those mats now that you are reading in your partnership?" Everyone agreed that the partners would read one book from one partner's mat, then one from the other.

"In a minute, you are going to read through your two stacks of books together, deciding whether to see-saw read or echo read. But first, will each of you find an easy book, that you really enjoyed, to read with your partner? Put it on the top of your stack. Then pick a super hard book, that you also enjoyed but may want some help reading. Put it on the bottom of your stack."

I let the children shuffle through their piles, and then said, "Readers, first read your easy books to each other. Read them and enjoy one another's books. Then when your reading muscles are warm enough, read your hard books together, helping each other figure out what your book is all about. You will have to use all your powers. As you read, make sure the *two* of you are working together to figure it out!

"After you do that, if you have more time, read through your piles. Get reading!"

Celebrate Persistence

Point out the strategies readers used to get through tricky parts of books.

"Readers, as I watched you read today, I could see your reading muscles growing right before my eyes. You are really becoming *stronger* readers! Let's read this challenging book together, and as we do, I'll show you some of the hard work I saw you doing today."

I opened the enlarged text and, with the class joining in, began to read. Turning to the second page, I halted the class with my raised finger, and said, "Wait! I'm remembering something *totally cool* that I saw earlier. Owen went like this," I said, as I moved my finger around the picture. "And only then did Owen read the words on page! What power was he using to read?" The class hollered, "Picture power!" "Owen didn't just look at the picture quickly. No way! He was really studying it, thinking about what was happening on the page."

I began reading again, and the class joined in. I then stopped suddenly, hitting my forehead. "Oh, silly me! Now it is coming back to me! Another thing I saw today is a whole *bunch* of kids reading this page like this," and I pointed crisply under the words. "How old are you?" I asked, scanning the room, as if I couldn't quite believe that these five- and six-year-olds were doing such advanced work.

"One reader even went like this." I pointed without one-to-one matching before going back to correct my mistake. I explained, "He noticed something wrong and fixed up his reading to make it match!"

We progressed through a few more pages of the book in the same way before bringing the session to a close. "Readers, I'm pretty sure that throughout the next few weeks, every one of you is going to do really hard work on all the pages of your books. I'm sure you'll be looking closely at the pictures and words on each page to help you figure out what is happening."

Session 2

Readers Use Patterns to Help Them Read Almost Every Page

MINILESSON

IN THIS SESSION, you'll teach children that figuring out the pattern can help them read their books.

CONNECTION

While convening the class, create a simple rhythm by alternating between two claps and two taps on your knees, recruiting kids to join into the pattern game after they are in the meeting area.

Before calling children to the meeting area, I asked them to get ready for reading. "Set out your reading mats," I said. "Make sure you pile your books so the easy ones are on top and the harder ones are on the bottom. When you are done, show me you are ready to come to the meeting area." I then called the tables of children to the meeting area. Right away, I provided percussion accompaniment, alternating between clapping my hands—clap, clap—and tapping my knees—tap, tap. Some children joined me once they'd taken their seat on the carpet next to their partner.

Point out that children's talent for figuring out patterns will help them read harder books.

Once everyone had gathered, I paused and leaned forward. "Wow! You all figured out that pattern, the parts that repeat, so quickly. And you know what? Figuring out patterns helps you read lots of books!

"Yesterday you noticed that in some books, there are more words, and the sentences are longer. But today I will give you a secret source of power that can help you. This is a very important secret, so listen carefully," I dropped my voice to a whisper and motioned for the kids to come closer.

❖ **Name the teaching point.**

"Today I want to teach you that even when there are more words on the page or the sentences are long, there is often a pattern in those sentences. And remember, if you can figure out the pattern, that pattern can help you read almost every page *and* help you know what your book is about."

GETTING READY

✔ Gather Unifix® cubes (or other multicolored manipulatives) for work with patterns (see Teaching).

✔ Select a demonstration text with a clear pattern at, or slightly above, the current benchmark level (B/C with a book introduction). We use *Picnic*, by Phyllis Root, but this text is interchangeable with others (see Teaching).

✔ Find a leveled book from the classroom library to use with a document camera if one is available. This book should have a clear pattern and a longer sentence structure than the book used in the teaching (see Active Engagement).

✔ Display the chart "We Are Super Readers!" and have the "We have pattern power" strategy ready to add to the chart (see Link).

✔ Choose a book from your library that features a see-saw pattern, one that goes back and forth across two pages (see Mid-Workshop Teaching).

✔ Be ready to rearrange the partner chart from the previous unit, and add a new Post-it®: "Play 'Guess What's Next!'" (see Transition to Partner Time).

✔ Prepare a class pattern book by assembling oversized paper into a five-page booklet. We chose to highlight children from the class reading and placed a photo of each child in the booklet ahead of time. The title, "We Like to Read!," was prewritten. Whatever topic you choose, use a pattern that see-saws, perhaps written across two lines of print per page. This pattern book will be used across the bend (see Share).

TEACHING

Explain to children that when they work hard to figure out the pattern, it will help them predict what is going to come next.

"Tell me something. Do you see a pattern here?" I laid out multicolored cubes in a simple pattern on the ledge of the easel: red, blue, red, blue, red, blue. The kids nodded yes. "Here's the harder question. When you read this pattern, can you figure out what comes next?" Again, the kids were confident: after red, blue, red, blue, red, blue they predicted red would come next. Then blue again.

"Are you ready to read something more challenging? Do you see a pattern here?" I made another sequence of patterned cubes: red, red, red, blue, blue, blue, orange. Red, red, red, blue, blue, blue, orange. The kids chimed in again with the next stretch of the pattern. "Wow! I can't trick you, and I don't think your books will trick you either. Figuring out the pattern helped you know what was coming next. It's the same in your books. If you work hard to get the pattern, you can read *any* patterned book."

Show how the children's understanding of patterns can be applied to a simple pattern book.

"Let's try figuring out what is happening in this book, together. Let's study and see if the pattern will help us!" I held up *Picnic*, by Phyllis Root. "Let me read the first three pages, and show me a thumbs up when you think you've figured out the pattern! Listen closely!" I read the first three pages aloud:

> *Mouse finds cookies.*
>
> *Mouse finds apples.*
>
> *Mouse finds bread.*

I made sure not to show the next page. "Wait! I see a lot of thumbs up! Do you think you've figured out the pattern already? If you *really* know the pattern, you will know what is going to happen next. Do you know what will happen next? Whisper it quickly to your partner!"

After a moment, I called the students back. "Listen to what I think, and see if it matches your guess. I think that Mouse is going to *find* something else to eat, like maybe a hot dog! Did anyone else think that? A lot of you saw that on every page Mouse was finding something to eat! Let's see if the next page will also say, 'Mouse finds' another something to eat. Read the next page with me." With the book under the document camera, I asked kids to chime in. "You were right! On this page, Mouse *also* finds something to eat. *And* this time, read it with me, 'Mouse finds *cheese*.' The pattern helped all of us read this next page, because we could easily guess what was going to happen next!

You will want to give students lots of practice recognizing and making patterns. You may want to work with patterns during math or at other times of the day so that students have lots of practice with patterns.

"Hmm, . . . Do you think Mouse will find a toy on the next page? No? A pet? No? What? You think he's going to find *another* kind of food, like rice? Let's see," I said, turning the page. "Oh! You're right!"

Name what you did in a way that transfers the skill to another text on another day.

"Readers, even when books seem challenging, you can read them because there is often a pattern that can help. If you can figure out the pattern, it can help you read almost every page."

ACTIVE ENGAGEMENT

Invite children to join you in a shared reading of one page of another leveled text, emphasizing that the sentences are long and that grasping the pattern (after reading page 1) really helps.

"Let's try this in a new book. We'll read the first few pages together. I'll go first, and then you reread with me. See if you can figure out the pattern and then guess what the next pages will say. When you know the pattern, put your fist up in the air like this." I raised my arm up strong, as if showing my muscles. "Ready?" The children nodded enthusiastically as I placed a new book under the document camera.

I began pointing under the words, inviting the class to read along. "Wow!" I said, looking up before the end of the second page. "Some of you think you already know the pattern! These sentences are long! Let's read on and see if more people can figure out the pattern to help read the rest of the book."

Set the children up to continue reading without your support, first for a page or two aloud and in unison, and then to whisper read as you continue turning the pages.

After reading two pages in unison, I said, "Ooo! Ooo! I think I know the pattern and what will happen next! Anyone else?" I raised my fist in the air.

Power fists shot up almost instantly. "Almost everyone sees the pattern here! If you know the pattern, it will help you know what is going to happen next and to read the next pages. Whisper to your partner how you think the next pages might sound." I let the students turn and predict, and then I voiced over to the whole class, "Say the words that you think you will see on the next page." I turned the page and said, "Whisper read with your partner and use the pattern to help you on the next two pages." I moved around the rug to coach students in doing this work.

LINK

Recap today's teaching and add to the chart from the previous unit.

"This is *amazing*! In just two days, you have read so many new books. I can't believe it. When your books get more challenging, remember the secret I shared with you today. Even when the sentences are long, if there's a pattern, you can figure it out! Then think about what is going to happen next. This gives you the power to read almost every page!

Plan to continue exposing students to lots of pattern books. You'll want to include books with strong patterns during both read-aloud and shared reading.

As your readers move from reading level A to level B books, they may find that there are more words per page than they are used to. While level A books will only have one line of text on a page, level B texts can have two lines on a page. For this active engagement, consider whether or not your readers are secure with a return sweep, moving back to the left on the next line of text.

"We've got to add that power to our chart!" I exclaimed as I gestured toward the "We Are Super Readers" chart from the previous unit and quickly added a new line.

We Are Super Readers!

- We have pointer power.
- We have reread power.
- We have partner power.
- We have picture power.
- We have snap word power.
- We have sound power.
- We have persistence power.
- We have book talk power.
- **We have pattern power.**

We have pattern power.

"Today, be sure to activate your pattern power," I said, putting my power fist in the air. "Especially when you read the harder books at the bottom of the pile on your reading mat." Picking up the Private Reading sign, I sent the children off to read. "Off you go, to read a *ton!* Off you go to learn a *lot!*"

Remind Kids to Draw on All They Have Learned Earlier

EARLY IN ANY UNIT, you'll want to get the new work underway while also reminding students to draw on all they learned earlier. It's common, then, to move extra quickly on the first day or two, likely doing some quick two- to three-minute "dip in/ dip out" conferences.

The first easy thing to support will be the use of reading mats. Reinforce the idea that books are piled so that the easiest books are on top. Once that routine is in place, notice what your readers are already doing, as well as the one "next thing" they *could* be doing, with a bit of help. For example, you may ask a student to read his book and then pause to celebrate his attentiveness to the pictures. "You are using the pictures to think hard about this book. That's so important! It shows you're a big thinker."

Then point out a next step, saying, "Can I give you a tip to make your reading stronger?" Of course, that next step will be different for different readers, and what's important is that it *is* a next step. If a child is reading level B books, for example, you aren't going to be as worried about accuracy. At this point in your children's development, it shouldn't be a big concern if a child has read *cookies* as *cake*, for example. This suggests the reader probably read with meaning (chances are good both words make sense), structure, and even an awareness of some visual information. If the child attends to first letters intermittently, remind her to make sure the word she says starts with the letter on the page.

Keep in mind that once readers are in control of making a return sweep, one-to-one correspondence, and using the picture as a source of meaning, they are ready to move to level C books (with a book introduction). That might mean your kids are ready to read level C books more quickly than you realize.

As you work on moving children into more challenging books, consider doing some small-group shared reading in instructional-level texts. Ask readers to pull up close to a little book. After a book introduction, read the text together, inviting students to join in the best they can. You will probably offer more support to your readers at the beginning of the shared reading, and then, as the book goes on, step back and let the kids take over more. Students can retell the book at the end. Then give each reader a copy of the text to add to his book baggie and read independently.

MID-WORKSHOP TEACHING
Readers Figure Out Trickier Patterns in Books

"Readers," I said from the middle of the room, "You're using patterns to read your books, and that is super! The thing is, patterns can be hard to figure out. Has anyone got a book with a *tricky* pattern?

"Listen to how *this* pattern goes: 'What color is your balloon? My balloon is red. What color is your balloon? My balloon is blue.' Wow, that is tricky! The pattern has *two* parts, and it goes across *two* pages! The first part is a question about the color. The second part is the answer. It's like the words on the pages are going back and forth, kind of like a see saw!"

I spread my arms out horizontally and reread the pattern, this time tilting my left arm down and then shifting the imaginary weight to my right arm as I read each part. "See? The pattern is like a see saw. Watch out! You, too, might have a see-saw pattern! If you can figure that out, then you can solve the next couple of pages. Like in this book, what will come next? That's right, 'What color is your balloon?' And I bet it will be . . . *orange*! Use the patterns in your books to read the best you can!"

TRANSITION TO PARTNER TIME **Play a Reading Game Involving Predicting Based on a Pattern**

"Readers." I flipped over our reading sign. "It's time for partner reading! And I have a fun game you can play with your partner.

"It's called 'Guess What's Next!' and it's all about figuring out patterns. Listen to the rules. One partner is the reader, and one is the guesser. The reader reads the first page but keeps the second page a secret. The guesser *guesses* what the next page *might* say. It's like guessing the pattern before you even know it! You have to pay really close attention to what is happening and what you are learning in the book to make a good guess! Check to see if the guesser was right. Then the reader keeps on reading, and after a few more pages, the guesser can try again. By now, you should know the pattern and have an even *better* idea of what the next page might say. Then change places: the guesser becomes the reader. This time, use a new book—the next one in the pile. You can go through your whole pile that way if you have time."

I quickly demonstrated the game before having students try it out with their partners. I then circulated among partnerships, coaching readers with the activity.

After a bit, I ended the partner reading time saying, "Readers, I think it's time for a new partner chart! I noticed that there are things you know how to do so well that you don't need a reminder. Like these!" I said, holding up the Post-its "Put your book in the middle." and "Read the pictures and the words." "You've grown so much as readers that you don't need these on the chart any more!

"I've rearranged our partner chart to match the reading work you can do with your partner. You choose *how* to read together, like see-saw and echo reading." I pointed to the revised chart. "You can also choose *things to do* as you read." I said, pointing to the bottom of the chart. We should also add 'Play "Guess What's Next!"' to that list." I added the new Post-it and I reminded, "Check the chart to plan your time together during partner reading."

ANCHOR CHART

Readers Read with a Partner

Decide how to read.

- See-saw read.
- ECHO, Echo, echo read.

Decide what to do.

- Add a pinch of you. (I think . . .)
- Give reminders to use POWERS!
- Hunt for snap words.
- Play "Guess What's Next!"

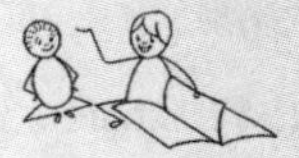

Play "Guess What's Next!"

Use Interactive Writing to Compose a Class Pattern Book

Share a patterned text with the class, and ask students to help you compose the next two pages.

"Readers *and* writers, last night, when I was lying in bed, a thought came to me: you've been reading all these new books by famous authors—but *you* are authors too! You've got writing folders *bursting* with your writing. So I thought, 'Maybe we could work together and write a new book—a pattern book—that could then go in *everyone's* book baggie!

"I was so excited about this idea that I got out of bed and I started the book!" I reached behind the easel for the book, holding it close to my chest, to keep the title a surprise. "This book is about kids who like to read, and *you* are stars of this book." I placed the book on the easel, lifted my pointer and read, gesturing for kids to join in. "Put your thumb up when you hear the pattern."

> ### We Like to Read!
> This is Ellie.
> She likes to read.
>
> This is Sophie.
> She likes to read.

"Has anyone figured out the pattern?" Hands shot up immediately. I reread the first two pages aloud to help the rest of the class hear the pattern, and soon more hands went up. "That's all I had time to write. I *did*, however, add one more picture." I turned the page, revealing another classmate's picture. They all called his name. "Will you and your partner think about how *this* page might go?" I prompted partners to turn and talk, rehearsing the language aloud. "Put a thumb up when you have an idea." Soon the class had dictated, "This is Devon. He likes to read." Picking up my marker, I said, "Okay, let's write it. Ready? Who can come up and whisper me some hints about what to write?" One child whispered, and I wrote, "This is . . ." "Devon!" the class filled in.

"What letter does Devon's name begin with?" I asked. The class replied, "*D!*" I prompted the class to point to this letter on the alphabet chart and write it on the carpet. Devon came up to the easel and wrote his name on the page. We added the second sentence to this page and then quickly moved to fill in another two pages. Across the next couple of days, I tucked Interactive Writing into other parts of the day to ensure that we had composed a page with each child on it.

FIG. 2–1   Class K105's interactive writing of a pattern book

Readers Figure Out the Changing Words in the Pattern

IN THIS SESSION, you'll teach children that they can use the picture and the first letter to solve unknown words.

GETTING READY

✔ Select a familiar favorite read-aloud that has a pattern. We chose to use *Pete the Cat and His Four Groovy Buttons*, but this text is interchangeable with others. *It Looked Like Spilled Milk*, by Charles Green Shaw, and *We're Going on a Bear Hunt*, by Michael Rosen, are other examples of texts you could use (see Connection).

✔ Select a level B or C demonstration text to enlarge under the document camera, if one is available. The text you use should have a repeating pattern, strong picture support, and opportunities to problem solve using the picture *and* the first letter or part. We use *Pizza*, by Phyllis Root (see Teaching and Active Engagement).

✔ Display the chart "We Are Super Readers!" (see Link).

✔ Have Post-its on hand (see Mid-Workshop Teaching).

✔ Letter-sound identification and high-frequency word lists (see Conferring and Small-Group Work).

✔ Have highlighting tape for isolating letters and words (see Conferring and Small-Group Work).

✔ Display your "Readers Read with a Partner" chart (see Transition to Partner Time).

✔ Prepare an interactive writing page that your class will use to add more pages to your demonstration text (see Share).

MINILESSON

CONNECTION

Point out that one of your students' favorite books is a pattern book. With the kids, sing your way through it, using the pattern to support fluency.

As children convened in the meeting area to the sound of "The Gathering Song," I sat holding a book in my arms, hiding the cover. "Readers, did you know that one of our *favorite* books is a pattern book?"

I quickly flipped the book over, and children chorused, "*Pete the Cat*!" "*Pete the Cat and His Four Groovy Buttons* is a pattern book! Can you turn and tell your partner how the pattern goes? What happens on each page?" The children started singing the pattern from the book.

After a few seconds I called them back together. "Yep! This cat talks about his buttons on each page!" I began bopping my head to the beat of the pattern while singing the repeated refrain from the story, "My buttons, my buttons, my four groovy buttons; my buttons, my buttons, my four groovy buttons. My buttons, my buttons, my—"

Stop abruptly at the place in the pattern where the word changes. Note that this changing word in the pattern is a source of challenge.

"ERRR!" I made a screeching sound like my car was coming to a halt. "Wait. Wait. Right there! *That's* where it changes. There's a new word there. That's where it changes from 'my *four* groovy buttons' to 'my *three* groovy buttons.' You know this happens in pattern books. In pattern books, each page doesn't say the *exact* same thing. Something changes on each new page, and it is the *same* kind of thing that changes. In this *Pete the Cat* book, the thing that changes is the number of buttons." And I resumed singing, "My buttons, my buttons, my three groovy buttons.

"So your job, when reading pattern books, is not only to know what is the same on each page but also what is *different*. That can sometimes be tricky! You'll be reading one page, and then the next page is similar (my buttons, my buttons), but then there is *one* thing that is different. (My four—Errr! My *three* groovy buttons!) Do you see, here, in the picture how it shows you *three* buttons? The word looks different too. Some people would have missed that! Luckily, you are readers who have the power to face this kind of challenge!"

❖ **Name the teaching point.**

"Today I want to teach you that when you get to tricky words in the pattern, think, 'What is the *same* and what is *changing* on each page?' Then you can look at the picture, think about what is happening, and get your mouth ready to say the first sound of the word."

TEACHING

Show children that readers carry the pattern from page to page and notice when there is a word that changes in the pattern.

"Let me show you how this goes as I read *Pizza*, by Phyllis Root. I'll pretend to be a kindergarten reader." I tapped the cover of the book, read the title, and thought aloud, "Oh, there's Mouse, right there on the cover, getting a pizza."

Tucking in a quick demonstration of habits readers do always, I made a point to quickly scan the picture before establishing the pattern in the book. "'Mouse makes toast,'" I read, pointing under each word. I read on to the next page with a sympathetic voice, "'The toast burns.'"

I turned the page. "Oh, look, it's a pattern! It looks like Mouse is making something else! That is the same. I began reading confidently, again pointing under each word. "'Mouse makes—' Errr!" My brakes screeched again. "*But* it's *not* toast! It's something different. This is hard. But I can do it!" I steeled myself for the challenge.

Model taking action to solve the word that changes in the pattern.

I took a deep breath, holding my finger under the word *soup*. "I'll look at the picture, right away, and figure out what is happening. Then I will get my mouth ready to say the first sound in the word," I said, smiling.

I searched the page and touched the part of the picture that was different from the page before. "Mouse is making . . . this thing!" Then, returning to the word, I said, "/s/, soup!" and many of the children solved the word along with me. "'Mouse makes soup.' That makes sense! Mouse is making soup. *And* do you see the /s/ sound in soup?

The book that is referenced in this minilesson will be used at other times during the bend. We chose a Pete the Cat *book because it is a favorite read-aloud that follows a pattern. Any engaging pattern book can be read to the beat of a song. The important thing is to find the place in the pattern where the word changes and draw students' attention to that unexpected word.*

"The word *soup* tumbled right out after I looked at the picture and I got my mouth ready to say the first sound in the word! And I'll continue to use the pattern on the next page: 'The *soup* burns.' Yes!

"Did you see how it helped to both study the picture *and* to get my mouth ready for that tricky word?" I leaned forward, making eye contact with the children, and they nodded in response.

ACTIVE ENGAGEMENT

Set children up to try out this work on another page, where the picture could be described by several different words.

"Readers, *you* try this out on the next page. Remember, you can expect a pattern, but not everything will be *exactly* the same. Pay attention to what you know about the pattern. Then you can look at the picture, think about what is happening, and get your mouth ready to say the first sound in the word. With your partner, read this page!"

I turned to page 5 and listened in as children word solved, encouraging them to reread once they'd figured out the page.

"Eyes on me, readers! I heard a lot of you read, 'Mouse makes . . .' because you know that part of the pattern is still on this page. *But* look, he's not making soup! He's making something different. Errr! But did you give up? No way! You looked at the picture, thought about what was happening, and got your mouth ready to say the first sound. Let's all read it together."

Our voices became one as I pointed under the words, 'Mouse makes *peas*.' So this next page must have *peas* on it too! Use the pattern and read it with your partner!"

After partners figured out the next page, I commented, "You sure brought your reading muscles to that challenge!"

LINK

Remind children to use both the picture and the first letter sound to figure out unknown words.

"Readers, remember that when you are reading your books and figuring out the pattern, your pages won't be *exactly* the same. Some things will be the same and something will be different! Be on the lookout for those changes. If you need extra help, you can look at the picture and, at the same time, say the sound of the first letter. Doing both of those things helps." Holding up the Private Reading sign, I sent the children off to start reading.

In this demonstration, you are showing students how they can use a variety of sources of information to figure out a word. You want students to be able to draw from the meaning of the text (often the picture), their knowledge of language structures (perhaps anticipating what word might come next), and visual information (at this level the first letter or part of a word).

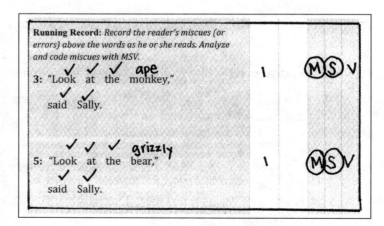

FIG. 3–1   This student is using meaning and syntax and needs to use visual as an additional source of information (initial consonant). Be on the lookout for readers like this.

Using Data to Plan Teaching

A S CHILDREN GO OFF TO READ INDEPENDENTLY, you'll want to do a fair bit of kid-watching at this point in the unit. Find a place in your classroom from which you can scan the room, watching as kids get out stacks of books and make plans to start reading.

In a one-minute scan, you can begin to notice how kids get started and who has trouble beginning right away. This will immediately tell you which students need support with initiating. At this time in the year, you will be balancing kids who are not yet conventionally reading with kids who are just beginning to do so. Trouble initiating their reading may be different in each of these circumstances.

If children who are not yet conventionally reading are unable to get started right away, make sure that they are supported with a book introduction. These children should also have lots of familiar texts available to them so that they can build stamina.

If children who are beginning to read conventionally are having trouble getting started, this may signal that the work of conventional reading feels tricky or scary, even if they can do it. You might suggest to these students that they begin with familiar texts as a warm-up or take a picture-walk in their new books so that they can get accustomed to the text before jumping in.

In addition, you'll want to use assessments, such as the letter-sound identification and high-frequency word lists, to plan for small groups. As you analyze your data, you should be on the lookout for kids who have not gained automaticity with a bank of high-frequency words and students who are still building letter-sound knowledge. Also keep in mind that these assessments record what kids can do with high-frequency words or letters and sounds when they are in isolation. Some children may show skills on these assessments and yet struggle to transfer their knowledge into actual reading. Your running records will help you identify students struggling with this.

You may decide to pull together a group of students to help them recognize familiar snap words in their books. You might say, "When readers see words they know in a snap, they recognize them every time! They recognize them on the word wall *and* in their books." You might start with a shared reading of the word wall and then coach each student to notice snap words in her own just-right books.

You might hold a similar small group for students learning to transfer all they know about letter sounds to the books they are reading. Gather these students and read through an alphabet chart together. Then you might say, "You are experts at knowing which letter makes which sound. You can do this when you read the ABC chart *and* when you come to words in your book that are tricky by making the sound the first letter makes out loud." Then as you coach kids in their just-right books, remind them that they can use the picture and the initial sound together to read unknown words.

> ## MID-WORKSHOP TEACHING
> ### Marking Challenges to Prepare for Partner Support
>
> "Thumbs up if you've found a pattern in your book! Okay! Thumbs up if you're checking the picture to help you! Great! Is anyone working hard to use the first letter at the same time? Wow!
>
> "Readers, I do need to tell you one thing. Sometimes, even when you use *everything* you know, you're still *really* stuck. When that happens, readers can get a little extra help from partners. You can use a little Post-it to mark a page that's super-duper challenging," I said, demonstrating quickly.
>
> "As you read, I'm going to come around and quickly give you each some Post-its to keep in your baggie. That way you'll be ready to work on those tricky parts with your partner. Alright, keep reading!"

I flipped the class reading sign over to signal that Partner Reading was in session. "Readers, it's partner reading time! Before you do anything else, decide how you will read your books." I pointed to the partner chart. "Will you echo read? Will you choose to do something as you read, like hunt for snap words or play 'Guess What's Next!'? Talk together and decide how to read your books."

After children talked, I continued, "Each one of you should have your books set up on your reading mat." I waited to make sure they made their stacks, organizing them in a loose progression of books from easier to harder.

"I already see some Post-its popping out of a few of your books. If you had some super-duper challenges in your books today, make sure you've marked the hard parts! There is a saying: 'When the going gets tough, the tough get going.' I know we have a lot of tough and strong partners who can work together to figure out those tough parts with the Post-its that call out, 'Help!'

"As you read today, when you reach a page where the reader left a Post-it that signals 'Help! I got stuck here!' please use all your powers to get past those hard parts together."

FIG. 3–2   Reading partners remind each other to use super powers.

Use Interactive Writing to Create a New Page for a Familiar Book

Guide children in adding more pages to a familiar book.

I sang the gathering song as children put away their book baggies and made their way to the meeting area. "Readers, you have been working so hard to figure out the pattern and the things that are changing in your books to help you read every page. I bet you could even do that work as *writers*!

"Let's have more fun with our book, *Pizza*, and add more pages! First, we'll reread and remember how the pages go back and forth like a see-saw." I read aloud the first few pages, inviting children to chime in and make the see-saw gesture. "Mouse makes toast. The toast burns. Mouse makes soup. The soup burns. Mouse makes peas." After I read "The peas burn," I paused.

"Quick! Think about how the pattern in the book goes." I gave the class a brief moment before I said, "Let's add *more* pages to this book. How might a new page go? What else might Mouse make?" The children piped up with tons of suggestions: "Macaroni!" "Rice!" "Popcorn!" "Cookies!"

"Let's start with popcorn," I suggested. "How will the sentence go? Say it like the book!" The children turned and talked, and when we reconvened I pointed for each word on our blank page as I rehearsed, "Mouse makes popcorn." Looking at the students, I asked, "What should we draw to help readers figure that word out?"

"Draw popcorn!" a few students offered.

I sketched a picture of Mouse popping corn and prompted students to draw a picture on the rug with their fingers. Then we wrote, "Mouse makes popcorn," together. I wrote the first words before inviting a child to write the initial consonant in *popcorn*. Then I finished writing the word.

When that page was finished, I asked "How will the next page go? Remember how the pattern see-saws."

"The popcorn burns!" the class chimed. "*The* is one of our snap words," I reminded the children, and they shouted out the letters in the word as I wrote them. Next, we found and wrote the /p/ sound and one child recorded it on the page. I wrote the rest of the word. We followed the same steps for the word *burns*.

We reread our new pages and then I pointed out that it was time for reading workshop to end.

FIG. 3–3   Class K101 made its own page to add to *Pizza* by Phyllis Root.

Readers Use All of Their Super Powers to Read Pattern Breaks in Books

IN THIS SESSION, you'll teach children to expect pattern breaks in their books and to use all of their strategies to read those parts.

GETTING READY

✓ Refer to the pattern book from the previous lesson's connection. We use *Pete the Cat and His Four Groovy Buttons* (see Connection).

✓ Select a patterned demonstration text with a pattern change at the end. We use *Picnic*, by Phyllis Root, but this text is interchangeable with others. You may choose to use a big book rather than using the document camera (see Teaching and Active Engagement).

✓ Display the anchor chart "We Are Super Readers!" (see Link).

✓ Prepare a final page for the class pattern book, "We Like to Read," which was started during the share in Session 2 (see Share).

MINILESSON

CONNECTION

Remind children of a favorite read-aloud in which the pattern broke at the end of the book.

"Readers, remember when we talked about *Pete the Cat* yesterday and we realized that it has a pattern that helps us to read almost every page? There is always a part that is the same on each page and then something that changes and is different." The children instantly started singing the pattern.

"Yes! 'My buttons, my buttons, my four groovy buttons. My buttons, my buttons, my three groovy buttons.' Then he has two, and then one button. But our *favorite* part is the ending! After Pete loses all of his buttons, Pete still has his . . ."

I waited, and the children chimed in, "Belly button!"

"That was a surprise, wasn't it? The pattern broke! Surprise endings are fun, but they can be hard work to read. We might need to bring *two* or *three* or even *every power* to the job!

"Just like when things got hard for Pete, you know that sometimes hard parts appear in your books. The words change on each page, and the patterns can change—sometimes at the end, sometimes in the middle—but when you get to those parts, do you cry? Goodness no! You keep . . . on . . . reading! You keep on reading, because you have strong reading muscles."

❖ **Name the teaching point.**

"Today I want to teach you that sometimes books can feel harder because the author tricks you! Books have patterns, and then—whoops! The pattern breaks! And it usually happens on the last page. Readers need to bring *every power* they have to solve that page."

TEACHING

Read to the end of a book to notice a pattern break. Then bring everything you know—all your reading powers—to read the last page, which is totally outside the pattern.

"Let me try it first. I'll read this book," I held up my copy of *Picnic*. "As I read, I'm going to be on the lookout for the page where the pattern breaks. It's usually the last page." I opened up to the middle of the book and read aloud:

> *Mouse finds cheese.*
>
> *Mouse finds strawberries.*

"Yes, there's the pattern. Mouse finds something on every page." I read on:

> *Mouse finds Dog.*

Then, I paused at the next page, scratching my head as if perplexed by the pattern break.

> *Dog finds a bone.*

"Wait! This page looks different. Thumbs up if you're noticing a pattern break, too." The class held up their thumbs. "I'm going to have to do some hard work to read this page. Should I cry?" I prodded.

"No!" the class chimed in.

"Okay, I'll need to bring all my powers to help me read this." I glanced at the "We Are Super Readers!" chart. "Yes! Picture power. I bet that can help me here." I peered back at the page. "Well, first of all, the picture looks different. On every page Mouse was in the picture, and now Mouse isn't there. But I see Dog. Hmm, . . . he's looking at a bone. It looks like this time *dog*, not *mouse*, finds something to eat."

Then I pointed to the first word. "Okay, time to activate pointer power. Don't help me, though. I want to do this *all* by myself. If you know it, put a thumb on your knee. *And* if you think you have an idea about the *powers* I should use, put a hand on your head. Ready? Here I go."

I tapped under the word *Dog*. "Hmm, . . . I don't think this says, 'Mouse.' I see some of you think you might know it. But if I want to do this *all* by myself, I'm going to need to use some powers to read this page. Hand on your head if you know what power I should try." Many children put a hand on their head to indicate they had suggestions. I looked back at the chart. "Do you think I should use reread power? How about sound power? Oh my goodness, maybe pattern power, too." The children nodded. "And snap word power," one voice called out.

One of the repeated refrains in Pete the Cat and His Four Groovy Buttons *is* "Did Pete cry? Goodness, no!" *after each of his buttons pops off. We adapt that here, aware that the children know the reference. If you haven't read* Pete the Cat and His Four Groovy Buttons, *you might say something here like,* "When you get to hard parts, will you worry? No way!"

I held my arms out in front of me, as if holding a stack of powers plucked from the chart. "Wow! All these super powers are getting *super heavy*. I better bring them over here and use them to read this page." I moved back to the text. "I see Dog in the picture. Oh! /d/ Dog." I pointed, once again, under the first word. "I see a *d*. Yes, this must be the word *dog*. 'Dog /fff/. Oh, the pattern was Mouse *finds*. Maybe now it's *Dog* finds." I reread. "'Dog finds—I see a *snap word*! 'Dog finds *a*." I tapped the picture. "A bone!"

"Will you reread this page with me now?" I pointed, leading the class in a choral reading of the page. "Whew! That was a lot of work. I needed to bring *so many* powers to help me read this page."

ACTIVE ENGAGEMENT

Set students up to work in partnerships to read the last page of your demonstration text, using all of their powers to tackle the pattern break.

"I wonder if the book will now tell all the things *Dog* finds," I pondered aloud, setting students up for another break in the pattern. I turned the page.

> Mouse and Dog have a picnic.

"Oh, no! This page looks very different. It's a *surprise* ending! Should we . . . *cry*?"

"Goodness no!" the class chimed back.

"Okay, readers. Remember to bring *all* the powers you know to help you read this page. Work with your partner to read it the best you can." I placed the last page under the document camera and moved around the room to listen in on the strategies students were using to read the page. I coached into the partnerships, as needed, reminding children to search more sources of information. "Don't forget to use the picture, too. Activate picture power! What are they doing? What do you see?" "Use snap word power to read that next word." "Check the first letter. Use sound power. What word might fit there?"

Recap the powers children used to figure out the pattern break, and then invite them to read the last page together.

I called the students back to read the last page together. "Wow, you are bringing *so* many powers with you to read this page. Picture power *and* sound power *and* snap word power!

"Let's read the ending together. I'll point, you read."

> Mouse and Dog have a picnic.

You'll want to move through the process thoughtfully, emphasizing the sources of information you're using to read the words. For example, notice that we model the process of searching for visual information, by saying "/d/ dog. I see a d. Yes, this must be the word dog." Then you'll search for meaning in the illustration by tapping on the picture to indicate how to arrive at the word bone.

You will want to listen in and coach readers to use all of their strategies as they try to read the page. Prompt students to integrate meaning, structure, and visual information.

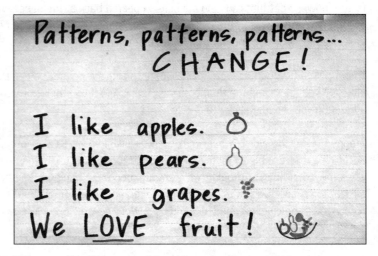

FIG. 4–1   Chart to support teaching of patterns

LINK

Remind children to be on the lookout for pattern breaks across their books.

"Readers, as you read harder and harder books, you are going to need to bring *every* power you have, especially when the pattern breaks! Be on the lookout for surprises. There will be *new* words on every page, and the pattern often breaks at the end of the book. Sometimes the patterns even break in the middle of a book. Don't get tricked!

"Let's reread our super readers chart so you can carry *all* of your powers back to your reading spots to use them today. Ready to carry them all? Arms out!" I turned to the "We Are Super Readers!" chart and read as the children chimed in. For each power, I acted as though I was lifting it off the chart and resting it in children's arms. Once we had read the chart, I raised the sign and sent students off to begin private reading time.

Pulling Small Groups with the Earliest Readers

ONCE A UNIT is well launched, you will want to turn your attention to making sure that your conferring and small-group work supports the kids who need extra help. At this point in the year, the readers who will concern you most will be those who are not yet using one-to-one correspondence, using known words to anchor their reading, or using letters and sounds as they read. Perhaps you'll plan a few small groups that can support students who need a toehold in these aspects of reading.

For starters, you may decide to support these readers in a guided reading group. Start by giving them a book introduction that helps them read a level A or B book. Then coach them in reading that text, ensuring that they are reading with one-to-one correspondence and checking the picture to make sure the words they read make sense. After you have coached these readers in this level A or B book, give them a copy to keep in their book baggies. Then send them off to read, saying, "Now, take out your other books and keep on pointing with your fingers and checking the picture to help you match to the words." You may want to refer to Session 8 for a more detailed explanation of guided reading.

You may also decide to do small-group shared reading with these students. Have students read along with you, taking turns to point at the words. After you read the book through once, you might return to it to do some additional work. For example, you might call on kids from the small group to locate isolated words, saying, "Now that we have read this page, Carolina, can you find the word *the?* Yes, now let's keep reading." Or you may prompt kids by saying, "Everyone, before we read this page, who can find some of our *snap words* on the page? Let's say them and then let's read the page!"

Practicing saying and finding sounds on the page may also be something you decide will be helpful to your students. When you return to reread a page, you might tell your readers, "Let's look for the word *flowers*. Everyone say, 'flowers.' What sound do you hear at the beginning? What letter is that? Let's find the word!" These sorts

MID-WORKSHOP TEACHING
Noticing Varied Punctuation at the End of a Book

"Readers, eyes up here," I said, standing in the middle of the room. "Thumbs up if you have found surprises in your books today." I looked around the room and saw thumbs popping up. "One thing that can help you when you are on the lookout for surprises is to look at the ending punctuation. If there is an exclamation point or a question mark at the end of the last sentence, that's often a signal that the author did something fun (and challenging) there. Make sure that when you are reading, if there is a question mark, you read it like *you* are asking the question. If there is an exclamation point, get your voice to read it with extra power or excitement!

"Okay, keep on reading!"

TRANSITION TO PARTNER TIME
Partners Coach Each Other When the Pattern Breaks

"Partners, it's time to double your powers and read together! Make sure your books are stacked, and remember to talk about how you will read together. Remember that you can help each other make your reading even stronger by reminding each other to use *all* of the reading powers you have, especially when the pattern breaks. Be on the lookout together for those pattern breaks, and then work together to read the new words the best you can!"

I flipped our sign from Private Reading to Partner Reading, saying, "Most of all, partners, as you read together, have fun. Read a *ton* and learn a *lot!*"

of book-based activities help readers understand the concept of a word, develop their knowledge of high-frequency words, and improve their ability to use letters and sounds as they read.

You might consider using writing to support reading by bringing students' writing folders into the reading workshop, suggesting that instead of reading books from the library shelves, they can read the books they have authored—or the books their friends have authored. Over a couple of days, you may decide to lead a short interactive writing group to help students who are well below benchmark work on labeling, hearing all the sounds in a word, and recording a letter for each sound. Do that work for several words and channel students to practice rereading the shared piece. Then you could have students do the same work in their own writing pieces.

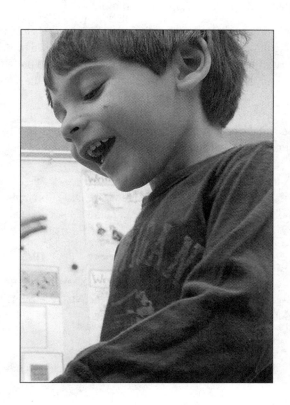

Shared Writing to Write a Pattern Break for the Ending of a Book

Reread the class book and encourage children to write an ending featuring a pattern break.

"Readers, you have been working so hard to notice the pattern breaks in your books and use *all* of your powers to find and read surprise endings in your books. You are really working through those hard parts and not getting tricked by the author." I leaned in and whispered, "I have an idea. Do you want to try to trick *your* readers? We could add a pattern break to change the ending of our class book. We could write a surprise ending together—a surprise ending to the book we wrote a few days ago. What do you think?" Everyone cheered. I placed "We Like to Read" on the easel.

"Well, before we write the ending, we are going to have to reread the beginning of the book together to remember the pattern. As we read, think about how we can break the pattern to make a surprise ending." Together, we read aloud the class book.

On the last page, I revealed a photograph of the entire class reading. "Look at the picture and think," I prompted. "What should we write to break the pattern and make the ending a surprise? Turn and tell your partner, quick!" I leaned in to collect a few possibilities before choosing one that would fit nicely—an ending that featured a pattern break, made sense, and included a few high-frequency words.

"Devon and Josephine had a suggestion: 'We love to read! Do you?' What do you all think? Does it break the pattern? Yes, it definitely does. Does it make sense with the picture? Yep, it does! Might it trick our reader? Yep, because now it's not just *one* student, it's all of us! It even asks the reader a question. Oooh, tricky!" I grabbed my marker. "Let's write it!"

We began a quick shared writing as students shouted out each word, chanting the letters of word wall words, and I recorded the words in our book.

> We like to read! Do you?

We reread our entire book when we finished. "Wow! What a great book we made together!" I said, turning back to the class. "I'll make sure everyone gets a copy to keep in their book baggies!"

FIG. 4–2   Class pattern book

FIG. 4–3   K105's shared writing of a pattern break at the end of the class book

Readers Check Their Reading

CONNECTION

Celebrate the idea that already in their lives, your children are careful problem solvers.

Before I called them over to the meeting area with our gathering song, I observed for longer than usual as the children set up for reading workshop, readying their stacks of books, securing their supply bins, and gently pushing in their chairs. When it was time to gather together, I marveled visibly.

"Wow. Readers, I feel so proud of the community we've built together here. This place," I paused, "is a place where people care and where people are care*ful*. I don't think it has always been this way, but as you've grown these past few months, you've become caring and careful; you've become problem solvers. When you see something is not right, you try to fix it! Like just now, I watched as Tyliek noticed one of our books on the floor, and instead of walking right past it, he asked a few friends if they were missing a book. And Grace found an empty juice box on the floor and she didn't yell 'Eww!' or call me over. All on her own, she got a tissue, picked it up, and tossed it in the trash."

"And she helped me pick my blocks up when they fell all over the floor at choice time!" added Sami, smiling. Grace beamed. "This class has so many stories of fixing things when they are not quite right.

"Well, listen, readers. Just like we don't *walk* right past problems in our classroom, we don't *read* right past problems in our reading."

I pointed to our new chart.

IN THIS SESSION, you'll teach children that even after they think they have solved the words, their reading work is not finished. You will show them that readers monitor for meaning and structure, and if their reading doesn't make sense or sound right, they must fix it up.

GETTING READY

- ✔ Prepare places to make several miscues in a demonstration text, without taking into account meaning or structural information. We chose to use the text *Cat and Mouse*, by Phyllis Root (see Teaching and Active Engagement).

- ✔ Display the chart "We Are Super Readers!" (see Conferring and Small-Group Work).

- ✔ Begin a new chart titled "Check Your Reading!" to teach readers to monitor their reading and fix mistakes (see Connection).

- ✔ Select a familiar text to retell. We return to *Cat and Mouse*, by Phyllis Root (see Share).

✤ Name the teaching point.

"Today I want to teach you that careful readers check that their reading makes sense and sounds like a book. They stop and ask, 'Did that make sense? Did that sound right?' If not, they don't just keep going! Readers try to fix it!"

TEACHING

ANCHOR CHART

Check Your Reading!

Ask:

Does it make sense?

Does it sound right?

Demonstrate monitoring for meaning and structure.
Make errors and be explicit about the questions you ask to check your reading.

"Watch and listen closely, readers. I am going to think out loud, so you can hear all the careful reading work I'm doing." I tapped on my head and then placed *Cat and Mouse* on the easel. "It's so important for me to keep checking that my reading makes sense and sounds like a book. If it doesn't, I can't keep going! I have to stop and try to fix it!"

After looking at the cover and reading the title, I opened to the first pages, pointed under each word, and read accurately:

> Mouse runs.
>
> Cat runs after Mouse.

Nodding contemplatively, I said, "Yup, that made sense. It makes sense that the cat, here, is running after the mouse," I said, pointing to the picture. "Yup, that sounded like a book, as well. Okay, I can keep going!"

On the next page, I substituted the word *you* for *under*. "Mouse runs *you* a fence. Okay, let me check again. Did that make sense?" I put one hand on my hip and the other on my head. "Does that sound right?" I continued, moving my hand from my head to my ear.

Mouse runs.

Demonstrate using a strategy to correct the miscue.

"No, no it doesn't. There isn't anyone but Mouse in the picture, and *you* doesn't even sound right there. I can't keep going. I have to try again . . . I know, I'll try picture power!" I searched the picture, touched the helpful part, and blurted, "Under! 'Mouse runs under a fence.' Does that make sense? Is the mouse running under the fence?"

You'll want to demonstrate the work of checking both when you read accurately and inaccurately to communicate the importance of always monitoring your reading. For structural miscues, you can use a different part of speech than the word on the page. For miscues around meaning, you can disregard the picture, perhaps substituting a word that doesn't make sense in the context of the book or page.

Consider using (and teaching) clear gestures to reinforce these monitoring cues. Movement will not only anchor students' memory of these cues, but also support their understanding of what to check for as readers. Whatever gestures you use here, be sure to use the same gestures each time you ask the questions.

"Yes!" the children replied, and I agreed. "Does that sound right?"

"Yes!" they repeated, and I added, "It does!" I put my finger under the word, articulated the first sound, and ran my finger under as I read it. "Now I think the next page will say 'Cat runs after Mouse,' because it follows the pattern!

"Readers, did you see how important it was to ask myself those two questions as I read? I had to check if the word I read made sense and sounded like a book. And if not, I tried again and fixed it up! Thumbs up if you saw all that *careful* reading!" Thumbs popped up all around.

ACTIVE ENGAGEMENT

Channel children to check and fix your reading.

"Now it's your turn! I'll read the next page and you help me check it. Will you ask, 'Does that make sense?' (touch your head) and 'Does that sound right?' (touch your ear).

> *Mouse runs up a hill.*

"Mouse runs up a *hot*." I stopped at the end of the page after I miscued. Many children put their hands on their heads. Others clutched their ears. "Oh, I see that you are asking those important checking questions. Does it make sense? Does it sound right?"

"No!" they answered. "Oh, hmm, . . . Work with your partner to try again and read the page." I circulated among the children, coaching them to activate their super powers. When I called them back together, I reported how many children used the picture and the pattern to figure out the page. "I heard many of you read, 'Mouse runs up a hill.' *That* makes sense and sounds right! You sure are careful readers. You checked and fixed my reading!"

I duplicated these steps on the final page of the book to give children repeated practice before restating the teaching point.

LINK

Remind children to check their reading and to try to fix it when it doesn't make sense or sound right.

"It's time to go off to read. I pointed to our sign. Remember, you are caring and careful readers! You don't want to miss what your books are about; you always want to understand what you are reading. Be sure to check your reading by asking yourself, 'Does that make sense? Does that sound right?" and if it does not, try to fix it up! Activate all of your super reading powers to figure it out. You can use the chart to help you. Off you go, problem solvers!"

While readers use three sources of information (meaning, structure, and visual information) when problem solving words, you'll notice that we have made the choice to highlight checking for meaning and structure. Though we did tuck in a tiny demonstration showing children how to check for an initial letter match, we didn't explicitly teach into this. We want to emphasize that, first and foremost, reading should always be meaningful! It is important that students have this in mind as they move into the second bend, with its focus on visual information. We then come back to the concept of "checking" in Session 12, this time showing children how they can check for all three sources of information.

Using the Anchor Chart to Reflect on Student Progress

AS YOU NEAR THE END OF THIS BEND, it is a good time to reflect on your students' progress and identify what it is that readers are ready to learn or need more support with. Use this information to inform your conferring and small-group plans not just for today, but also for the next bend in the unit. You can use the "We Are Super Readers!" anchor chart as a guide when you are looking over your conferring notes and observing readers. This is a good time to check to see if students are:

◆ Matching spoken words to printed words

◆ Using the illustration and the story as a source of information

◆ Using the pattern as a source of information

◆ Making a return sweep on more than one line of print

◆ Reading known high-frequency words in text automatically

◆ Using the beginning part of the word along with meaning and structure

You will also want to follow up with the students you met with yesterday, supporting these readers through guided reading or other small groups across a series of days.

It is likely that you will have a group of students who are reading level B and easier level C books, who are using the illustrations and their knowledge of language (meaning and structure) but aren't consistently attending to an initial letter. These children might read, "This is a bunny." when the text says, "This is a rabbit." One reason that some readers find moving into level C books a challenge is because they need to begin to use more visual information, looking closely at the text.

MID-WORKSHOP TEACHING
Celebrate Students' Self-Monitoring

"Readers, can I have your eyes and ears?" Once I had the students' attention I began, "The absolute best thing I heard over the last fifteen minutes is this—listen up. It may sound funny, but the very, very best thing I heard was a few of you saying, 'Oops'!

"Hmm, . . . You know that *oops* means 'Oh, no! I made a mistake.' So why on earth do you think I am thrilled to my tippy-toes with hearing you say, 'Oops'?

"This is why: I am thrilled because this means you checked yourself. It means you caught your own mistake, and so you said, 'Oops,' and *oops* means, 'Let me try again.' So keep reading, and keeping saying, 'Oops' whenever something is not quite right."

TRANSITION TO PARTNER TIME
Partners Can Monitor Each Other

"Readers, how many of you caught a mistake in your reading today and said, 'Oops!'?" A few hands went up. "Hurray! Those 'oopses' can help you make your reading stronger so that you can go back and try again.

Sometimes, though, you're working *so* hard to read the words that you don't notice when there's an oops. You don't realize you made a mistake. Guess what! Partners can check to make sure that the words you are saying match the book so that your reading makes sense and sounds right. So, partners, take a turn being the 'oops checker' today. Listen closely to your partner read and check that his or her reading makes sense and sounds right. If not, say, 'Oops! Try that again.'"

Gather these students together for small-group shared reading sessions of level B and C books. You may want to help this type of reader attend to the first letter of words in level B books before moving to level C. Since this is a small-group shared reading session, choose a book you have multiple small copies of. This will enable you to hand a copy of the book to each student at the end of the small group.

Warm up for the shared reading by reading the class alphabet chart together. Then, before reading, support meaning by reading the title and discussing the front cover and gist of the book. During the shared reading, play "Guess the Covered Word" by using Post-its to cover two or three words in the text. As you encounter these words while reading, prompt readers to think about what would make sense and sound right when they are guessing what the covered word might be. The readers should think about and share the letter they would expect to see at the beginning of the word. You might uncover the initial letter before you uncover the whole word, providing a scaffold to support children to use the initial letter. As you continue reading, prompt children to use the picture and the first letter to problem solve words. At the end of the reading, do a quick comprehension check and restate the work the children were doing so it is generalizable and transferable to other texts.

It is also likely that you will have students who can read high-frequency words in isolation but need support with reading and writing these words in continuous text. You will want to gather these students with their book baggies and coach them to watch out for the words they know. You can also support these readers during reading workshop and throughout the day with interactive writing sessions in which children "share the pen" on high-frequency words they have learned. You can use high-frequency words to turn one-word labels around the classroom into sentences such as "Here are the books." or "Here is the flag." Remember that these labels can be changed throughout the year.

Readers Check Their Reading with a Retell

Teach students to use the title, pattern, and ending to retell a book.

I called students back to the meeting area. "Readers, you have been learning how to check yourself and say, 'Oops! I need to fix that.' You don't need me to check your reading. You do that all by yourself! But did you know there is another way you can check yourself? After you read a book, see whether or not you can retell it to yourself or someone else. If you can, that means you probably understood it pretty well. You can go back to the cover and use the title and the pattern to retell the book. Let's try that."

I took out *Cat and Mouse*. "Let's pretend that I just finished reading this book. But did I understand it? Do I remember it? I'm going to check by seeing if I can retell how the whole book goes.

"Remember, when we retell, we can think about how the title and the pattern and the ending go together! Like this: This story is called *Cat and Mouse*. Mouse runs to lots of different places, and Cat runs after him. At the end, Cat tags Mouse and it is Mouse's turn to run after Cat!"

I prompted the class to retell a book from their baggie to a partner, using the title, pattern, and ending to help them retell. I then brought the group back together and said, "Remember, whenever you read a book, you can check that you understand it by retelling it to yourself or a partner!"

Readers Use the Pattern and the Ending to Understand Their Books

---

MINILESSON

CONNECTION

Celebrate the work readers have been doing to become stronger, and especially note their newfound pattern power.

As I moved to the meeting area, I began singing the gathering song that had become a class favorite. The children joined in and gathered at the meeting area.

I leaned forward and said, "Last night, I was thinking about you and your reading muscles. See, I have a neighbor—Troy—who is about eighteen years old, and he goes to the gym to work out every day. He has giant muscles on his arms and legs," I said, using my hands to show Popeye-style muscles. "He told me the way he gets those muscles. Each time he tries, tries, tries hard to lift a heavy barbell, that hard work gives him a little more muscle. So day by day, he gets stronger and stronger.

"Listening to him, I realized that the way you have been trying so hard to read all the super books in this classroom has given you muscles like his—only yours are *reading* muscles.

"And I think the way you are working hard to notice what stays the same and what changes in patterns has especially given you more muscle, more power. Thumbs up if you think so as well."

Thumbs popped up in the air.

"Well, when readers become pattern experts, they don't just use the pattern to help them read the words in their books. They can also use all their new strength to better understand their books and talk about them."

IN THIS SESSION, you'll teach children that they don't just use the pattern to help them read the words; they also use the pattern and ending to better understand their books.

GETTING READY

✔ Select two texts at, or slightly above, the current benchmark level (B/C with a book introduction). We use *It's Super Mouse!* and *Pizza*, by Phyllis Root, but these texts are easily interchangeable with others. You will want to choose familiar patterned books with a pattern break at the end. You may choose to use big books or project smaller copies of texts using a document camera (see Teaching and Active Engagement).

✔ Ensure that students have Post-its in their book baggies (see Conferring and Small-Group Work).

❖ Name the teaching point.

"Today I want to teach you that pattern power doesn't only help you read the words in your books, but it can also help you *think* about your whole book. When you get to the last page of a book, you can think about how the ending goes with the pattern. Then ask, 'What is this *whole* book *really* saying?'"

TEACHING

Use a familiar text to demonstrate how you stop at the end of the book to use the pattern, and the way the pattern progresses across the book, plus the ending, to grasp what the whole book is about.

"Watch. When I get to the end of this book, I won't just close the book and pick up a new book. No way! When I get to the end, I'll use the pattern and the ending to think about what this *whole* book is *really* saying." I picked up *It's Super Mouse*, placed it under the document camera, and began to read. "Oh yes! I remember how this goes. Now I can use the pattern to read every page." I read to the end of the book and closed it abruptly.

"Wait! I am at the end. *Now* I can think a little more about the book. Let me use the pattern and the ending to think about what this *whole* book is *really* saying. Give me a thumbs up if *you* have some ideas." Thumbs went up.

I picked the book up and flipped through the pages quickly as I thought aloud. "Oh, he's jumping off so many things. On *every* page he jumps off something. First he jumps off a step, then a box, then a rock, then a fence, then a hill! Oh my goodness! The things on every page get higher and higher! Maybe that's why he falls at the end. He tried to jump off something that was way too high! Mouse wants to be Super Mouse and fly, but he crashes into the ground instead. Were some of you thinking that too?" The children giggled and nodded.

Recap the work you just did as a reader in a way that is transferable to another book, another day.

"Wow! The pattern really helped me think about this book. Did you see what I did? After I finished reading, I stopped to think about what happens on *every* page, especially at the end, and asked myself 'What is this *whole* book *really* saying?' That really helped me understand my book."

ACTIVE ENGAGEMENT

Channel the children to do this work with partners in another text that is familiar to the class.

"Do you want to try? First, we'll read the whole book. Remember, the pattern can help. When you finish, stop to think about the ways that every page is the same and how it changed at the end. That way you can use the pattern to help you answer, 'What is this *whole* book *really* saying?'

"It's another book about Mouse," I said as I placed the book under the document camera.

Notice the deliberate choice to reread a familiar book from the previous unit. You'll want to be sure to demonstrate the importance of rereading. Much of the work your children do will come after they read the book the first time, and you want to stress early on that when they finish a book, they don't just toss it aside. Instead, they think about what they read and reread it for more meaning.

You'll want to keep kids engaged across your demonstration, prompting them to think along with you. Notice how these children are prompted to silently participate in the teacher's demonstration, using gestures such as putting a thumb up when they have an idea. Avoid inviting students to share out loud, or in partnerships, however, because you'll want to be mindful of pace and the explicitness of your instruction. They'll have an opportunity to practice the strategy soon enough.

"*Pizza*!" the children cheered.

"I know, it is another one of our favorites! Remember, in this book, Mouse tries to cook things and burns everything, so at the end, he orders pizza. Let's first read it quickly, and then we can think about how the pattern helps you understand the *whole* book." I placed my pointer finger under the title and began reading aloud. The class chimed in, commenting and reacting every time we read about something else that mouse burned.

When we reached the end, I started to close the book and then dramatically caught myself, reminding the class that the plan was to recall the way the pattern goes on every page and then think "What is the *whole* book *really* saying?"

I returned to the beginning and began turning the pages, saying "What are you thinking?" After a moment, there were thumbs in the air. "It looks like you have some ideas you want to share with your partner. Turn and talk with your partner about what you are thinking."

The children turned and began talking with their partners. I moved around the meeting area, using this time to listen to partners and support children as needed. When I heard partners solely retelling what happened in the book, I prompted them to think more. I stopped at various partnerships and prompted, "What do you think about the ending? How does the ending go with the pattern? Do you have any other ideas? Say more about that."

Recap in a way that elevates students' responses.

"Readers, wow! Your pattern power is getting so strong. It is really helping you think and talk about your books. I heard some of you saying that Mouse was really hungry, so he tried to cook and he burned everything. He burned the toast, soup, *and* peas. Goodness! He was hungry and didn't want to keep burning things, so he ordered pizza! Now he won't be hungry. Maybe he should have just ordered pizza instead of trying to cook."

LINK

Point out that noticing patterns can help readers think and talk about the whole story.

"Readers, when you know how something goes, you can think and talk about the whole big thing. Like, for example, think about the patterns in our reading workshop. How does reading workshop usually go? Thumbs up if you have some ideas for the pattern of how reading workshop goes." Thumbs went up, and I said, "Tell the person near you about the patterns in reading workshop time." The room exploded into talk.

"When you see those patterns, you can talk about the whole of reading time. You can say things like 'Reading time is whole group, then one-to-one, then two-by-two, then whole group again.' Or 'I think reading time and writing time are practically the same.' That's thinking about the *whole* reading workshop. You do the same thing when you think about the patterns in your books. You can use the pattern to think about the whole book." Holding up the Private Reading sign, I gestured, "Off you go!"

This is critically important to express to your students—that the work of reading is not only in solving words, but also in comprehending their books.

Follow-Up Sessions with Readers

REMEMBER THE IMPORTANCE of following up with students on things you have already taught. You might, therefore, take a moment to look over your notes from the week so that you can follow up with individual conferences and small groups. To gather yet more data, you could begin most of your conferences and even your guided reading groups by asking a child to read aloud for you. The information you glean from observations, combined with your notes from prior instruction, should help to steer your work with individuals.

If you observe a child doing things you taught earlier in the week, you will probably want to name what you see. You can start with "I notice the way you . . ." and add how it is helping the reading. For example, "I noticed the way you got to the ending, paused, and turned back to reread some pages. That is helping you think more about your book!"

During this bend, you might have been working with readers reading level E books who were beginning to look across words and use word parts, and who needed to be reminded to rely on meaning. For a few days, you coached these readers by saying things like "Think about what is happening," and "Reread. Think of a word that would make sense." You will want to check in with these readers to see how they are progressing and make plans for their next steps.

It is also important to confer with your stronger readers. A handful of your kids may have begun kindergarten reading conventionally, and by now may even be reading levels G, H, I, or even J! Don't make the common mistake of underestimating your young readers. When in doubt, conduct a quick running record, and as soon as you've ascertained that a child is capable of reading higher-level books, be sure to help her

---

MID-WORKSHOP TEACHING   Readers Reread in Their Best Voices to Show They Understand

"I want to remind you that when you get to the end of your book, you don't just put the book down and start a new one! Remember, readers think about the book. They use the pattern to think about what happened on every page—especially the last page—to understand the book better.

"Guess what else? When you *understand* the book better, you can *read* the book better. You can go back and read the book again—this time with your very best reading voice to show you understand what the book was about."

I held up *It's Super Mouse* to demonstrate. "We know this book is all about Mouse jumping off things because he *really* wants to fly. So now I can read it again with an excited voice to show how much Mouse wants to fly." I opened up the first page and read it enthusiastically.

"Try that now. Pick up a book you've already finished. Now think, 'What was this *whole* book about? What happened on every page?'" I paused, giving children a moment to try this work in their own books. "Now reread in your *best* reading voice. Go!"

TRANSITION TO PARTNER TIME
Partners Can Give Book Introductions

"It's just about time to read with partners. Remember that you can introduce books to each other *before* you read together. Be sure to say the title of the book and then use the pattern to say what the book is all about. You might even point out a tricky part before you read. Then you can read that book together. Get started! Decide who will begin and introduce your books!"

---

fill her book baggie, and provide her with the kind of reading work that will keep her growing stronger and stronger.

In levels A–F, your children became accustomed to being able to rely on very strong picture clues. Chances are that whenever a word needed to be decoded, or posed any extra challenge, there was a picture there to support it. In levels G on up, this is not always the case. You'll need to teach these stronger readers some strategies for figuring out the story when the picture doesn't show much. For example, kids will need to think more carefully about what exactly is happening, even as they move from sentence to sentence.

As text complexity increases, so does the complexity of the story, so your readers will benefit from stopping from time to time to check for understanding. Have your readers retell what has happened so far. Prompt them to go back to the last place where things were making sense to reread if they lose track of the story. For example, "You don't want to get all the way to the end of these longer books without stopping to think along the way!" you might say to these readers. You might even teach some children to prepare their books before they read by placing small Post-its on pages where they plan to stop and retell to check their comprehension.

Celebrating by Giving Reading Gifts to Partners

Suggest that readers give their partners the gift of reading by introducing, reading, and swapping books with one another.

I invited the children back to the meeting area, asking them to bring along their book baggies. Once they had settled, I began, "Do you remember when we celebrated the super reading work you did and gave the gift of reading?" The children nodded, some shouting out who they read to at home. "Yes! That was *so* special. You are readers, after all, *super* readers, in fact. And, here's the best part: *you* can give reading gifts all the time. You can find books you love the most and read them in ways that get your friends and family to love them, too. You might even give them the book to read on their own. Right now, I bet there's a book in your baggie that you might like to read and give as a gift to your reading partner. Quickly choose one and put it on your lap." I waited a moment for children to make their selections.

"Now, Partner 1 will give a gift of reading first. You can give your partner a book introduction, then read the book with your *best* reading voice to show that you understand the book, and help your partner understand it, too. Then, you can *give* that book to your partner so he or she can add it to his or her own baggie and read it during private reading time. Then Partner 2 can give a gift of reading. Ready? Get gifting!" I moved proudly around the meeting area to listen in, complimenting all the reading work partners were doing.

FIG. 6–1   Chart to support partners giving book introductions

Readers Use Their Letter-Sound Knowledge to Help Them Read the Words on the Page

IN THIS SESSION, you'll teach children that one of their biggest sources of power is their letter-sound knowledge.

GETTING READY

✔ Use a piece of student writing as a demonstration text. You can use page 1 of Sam's story, covering the second sentence. This writing piece will be used in this session and the next (see Connection). ☚

✔ Select an alphabet book that is arranged by letter sounds (see Teaching).

✔ Prepare your "With ABC Books, Readers Can . . ." chart to remind children of the things they can do with their alphabet books. This chart will be used for today's launch and in the following session (see Active Engagement, Mid-Workshop Teaching, and Transition to Partner Time). ☚

✔ Pull together a collection of alphabet books for each child to access during independent reading (see Teaching).

✔ Have your alphabet chart available to reference, and check to make sure the children have their small copies in their book baggies (see Mid-Workshop Teaching and Share).

✔ Display your "Readers Read with a Partner" chart (see Transition to Partner Time).

MINILESSON

CONNECTION

Tell a story about a child who worked hard to record letters for all the sounds he heard in his piece of writing. Suggest that writers take care to record sounds because readers need those letters and sounds to read.

I sat in the meeting area, holding a piece of a child's writing to my heart. "I wanted to start reading workshop today by talking about writing workshop. I know that seems funny, but I have been thinking about how you all have been so thoughtful, hearing all the sounds you can hear in a word and writing a letter for each sound so that other people will be able to read your writing.

"I remember watching Sam, a kindergartner in this class last year, writing like this." Pretending to be Sam, I role-played writing and saying quietly, "I saw my BIG . . ." I then said *dog* over and over, stretching the word to hear all the sounds and complete the sentence.

"Here's the thing," I added. "Sam and all the writers in this room listen to hear every sound because you know that readers will need to look carefully at the letters to read those words. We needed Sam to write the letter *d* to tell us it wasn't a /b/ bear or a /p/ puppy, but his *big* dog! As books get more challenging, you will need more and more sound power."

❖ **Name the teaching point.**

"Today I want to teach you that one way to get stronger as a reader is to think and talk and play and sing with the alphabet, getting to know all the fun ways that letters and sounds go. Then when you read, you can use all you know about letters and sounds to read the words the author wrote."

TEACHING

Launch an exploration into alphabet books that will replace regular reading for the day (and perhaps be continued in word study time).

"Readers, I thought that today I'd show you a few great ways to read ABC books, and then maybe some of you can invent even *more* totally fun ways to read them. Today you'll get to spend the whole reading time working with ABC books! How does that sound?"

As the kids looked at each other and back to me, wiggling with anticipation, I pulled forward a basket brimming with alphabet books. I took one out as if it was a miraculous gift. "Let's look together at this alphabet book and think about how these books go. Before we even open this book, think to yourself, what do you think we will see on every page?" I paused. "Now whisper what you're thinking."

"Letters!" "A letter!" "The alphabet!" the students whispered.

"Yes! Some people call these alphabet power stations because readers can go to them to get more letter and sound power. But to get that power, you don't just read, read, read the book. Instead, you use the book to help you think about letters and sounds.

"Just like always, I'm going to look carefully at the pictures in my book to figure out how it works. Here is the first page. In this book, each page shows a letter and a few pictures of different animals whose names begin with that letter. Watch how I use the letters and the sounds to help me figure out the names of the animals on each page.

"A!" Using letters and the picture, I read, "A is for alligator." Then I got stuck on the second picture, which looked to me to be a monkey (although it was an ape), so I read, "A is for . . . monkey?

"Huh?" After pausing thoughtfully I said, "Let's try another way that *a* can sound" and this time generated "A is for ape."

FIG. 7–1   Sam's story with the second sentence covered

Many kindergarten teachers launch the year reading alphabet books to expose students to letter names and sounds. This will be a great time to revisit some of these books to study and read, focusing on using letters and sounds to read the words in books.

Your alphabet book can have an entirely different pattern. Just adapt this to suit whatever book you use.

Debrief, naming what you demonstrated that is transferable to other books and other letters.

"Do you see what we did, readers? We read the letter and used what we know about that letter's sounds to figure out why the author put those particular things on the page. When we thought the author had a monkey on the *A* page, did we just go 'Oh, well'? No! We worked with the picture—plus what we know about letters and sounds—to figure it out."

ACTIVE ENGAGEMENT

Distribute one alphabet book to each partnership and channel partnerships to read, figuring out why the author has chosen to illustrate each letter with the accompanying objects.

"Right now, will you and your partner read your alphabet book, remembering to use the letters and sounds, and to figure out why the author put those objects on that page? Get started!"

As partners worked, I moved among them, helping them to notice when letters made two sounds and to move on when they had read one page. "Some of your letters make a few sounds! How cool that you noticed that!" I voiced over to the whole class as they continued to work.

Add Ask, "Why this picture?" to the new anchor chart. Share a second way to read ABC books, also adding that to the chart.

Convening the class, I said, "So let's put this way of reading alphabet books on our chart, and I'm going to show you another way you can read these books." I revealed the new chart and added two bullets.

> **ANCHOR CHART**
>
> With ABC books, readers Can . . .
>
> - Ask, "Why this picture?" (Why ape for A?)
> - Play "Guess What's Next!"

Pointing to "Guess What's Next!" I reminded children that this is the title of a game they already played, involving using the patterns to predict. "Let's play it with this book," I said. I reread the first page of my demonstration text, noting that both the objects on that page were animals: the alligator and the ape. "Maybe on every page there will be a different kind of animal. We are going to think about what letter comes next and then guess what pictures and words will go with the letter. Guess what comes after this! Use your pattern power and your sound power! Tell your partner what you think."

Many kindergarten classrooms devote a few weeks to inquiries revolving around alphabet books, with kids making their own books (in teams so the effort doesn't become all-consuming). You may want to do this work during word study time or extend today's session by another day. If you decide to make alphabet books, copies of these books could be added to your classroom library as part of the celebration at the end of this bend.

If you can't secure enough alphabet books to supply one for every partnership, you can convene kids into groups comprised of two partnerships and then present one book to every group of four. These books are easily shared.

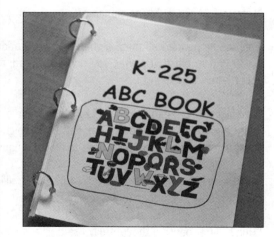

FIG. 7–2 Alphabet book cover

As children talked, I listened in briefly to a sampling of partnerships and then brought the group together. "Wow, great work using all your reading powers to guess what's next! I heard kids guessing letter *b* would be next. And that maybe there would be animals that start with *b*, like bears, bats, or birds. Thumbs up if you thought of that, too. I also learned something from you while I was listening in to you. I learned that it *can't* show bananas on the next page. Why not? Because bananas are not animals, of course!"

LINK

Explain that today's reading workshop will be different than usual because everyone will read ABC books, not books from their baggies, and because children will read in partnerships from the start.

"Readers, we are definitely learning more about letters and sounds. Alphabet books help us do that. They are like alphabet power stations because you can go to ABC books to get more sound power. And when you learn more about letters and sounds, it helps you read your books!

"Let's build up our sound power by reading ABC books for the whole reading time today! You won't have private reading time and then partner reading time. Instead, you and your partner will read ABC books. You won't need your book baggie today, just your ABC books.

"You have choices for how to read your ABC books with your partner. How many of you are going to read your book all the way through, A to Z, figuring out what the words are on each page and why they are there?" Many children signaled they would do this, so I sent them off with their partners. "How many of you are going to keep on playing 'Guess What's Next!'" I sent those readers off with their partners. "How many of you aren't sure what you will do?" I kept those readers with me and got them started.

FIG. 7–3   Bin of alphabet books ready for students

Working with Alphabet Books

I**T HELPS TO BE ABLE TO ANTICIPATE** the work that students are doing today and ways that you can ramp up that work with individuals and small groups. That's especially important today because you have launched a new bend, and done so by creating an out-of-the-ordinary day. You'll note that we suggested that students work in partners for the first portion of reading time and then in groups comprised of two partnerships for the second half of the reading workshop. We made that suggestion with the expectation that kids will devote the entire reading workshop to work with alphabet books, and we figured you probably don't have enough books for each student to have his own book. But, of course, you could deviate from the suggested plan—perhaps just asking kids to take a bit of time reading their alphabet book before shifting to work in their book baggie.

In any case, if kids are working in pairs with alphabet books for the first half of reading time, you'll want to get around the room quickly to make sure they know some ways to read these books. Encourage kids to be inventive. We've seen kindergarten children adding their own illustrations on Post-its to many pages. We've seen them deciding on their favorite page from the book. Certainly lots of children have enjoyed playing "Guess What's Next!" with the reader peeking ahead to see how the author illustrates a letter and the partner guessing possible items.

As children do this work, keep in mind that you are going to help them read the words in the books—not an easy job—and to do that, you'll encourage them to notice more letters, remembering that writers put all those letters onto the page so that readers can use them to figure out the words. Help readers to look at beginnings and move their eyes to the ends of words, and to realize that many letters make more than one sound. Your goal is for readers to be more flexible with their knowledge.

Those children in your classroom who are reading levels G, H, or above, will likely still enjoy the alphabet book work. But you may want to differentiate for them so they are provided with enough work to keep them growing and moving as readers as the rest

MID-WORKSHOP TEACHING
Inventing New Ways to Read ABC Books

I stood near the chart listing fun things readers can do with ABC books and said to the class, "Oh, my goodness! You have already invented more fun things to do with these books. One partnership is using Post-its to add their own pictures and words—to every page! So, if you are on the *d* page, you can think together, 'Do you know other words that sound like /d/?' And if the book has animals on every page, then you have to think about words that start with a *d* and are the names of animals. Like a dalmatian and a dachshund! Thumbs up if you and your partner might like to try that. Go ahead, keep reading and learning!

"Another partnership wasn't just reading the alphabet. They were *singing* it. Every time they turned the page, they went back and sang the alphabet song up to the new page." I added those ideas to the chart. "Before you do any of these things, though, will you swap books with a different partnership so you are reading a whole new ABC book?"

ANCHOR CHART

With ABC books, readers can . . .

- Ask, "Why this picture?" (Why ape for A?)
- Play "Guess What's Next!"
- Add more words.
- Sing the words!

Reading ABC Books Together in Many Ways

"Readers, can I have your attention?" I said, and waited until the excitement had quieted a bit. "Will you be sure that you get your alphabet charts out so you have them with you as you read? With your alphabet charts and your ABC books combined, you've really got your own alphabet power stations now! That's going to help you grow your sound power!"

As children did that, I said, "Watch as I go around the room and pinch partnerships together into groups." I circled, using my fingers to gesture that I was putting partnerships together.

"For the rest of reading time, you can work in these groups and you can use not just *one* but *two* ABC books. And I want to suggest one more really fun thing you can do when the four of you and your books start working together. You can think, 'How are they the same? How are they different?' The game is called 'Same and Different.'

"You can go to any page, starting with *a* or starting with the first letters in your names or anything, and then look at whether the books have any of the same ways to illustrate a particular letter. Then you can go to another page and see."

ANCHOR CHART	With ABC books, readers can . . .

With ABC books, readers can . . .

- Ask, "Why this picture?" (Why ape for A?)
- Play "Guess What's Next!"
- Add more words.
- Sing the words!
- **Play "Same and Different."**

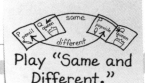

Play "Same and Different."

of the class works with these books. You might be able to gather enough alphabet books at levels that are just right for your higher readers. Or you might pull together a small group and have them work with alphabet books that teach information on a topic, highlighting comprehension. For example, you might teach into determining importance and main ideas. (What can we learn from each of these books? What is important on this page/section? What is not so important? What is each book mostly about?) Alternatively, you could have these readers spend a few minutes enjoying alphabet books before moving on to their just-right books.

As on any day, you will want to spend your time conferring one to one as well as working with small groups. Ensure that you continue to meet with guided reading groups across a sequence of days to support students as they move into new levels of text.

Boosting Phonological Awareness to Support the Visual Cueing System

Remind readers to bring their alphabet charts, and introduce a game to encourage identification of initial consonant sounds.

"Readers, come to the meeting area and bring your ABC chart!" Once children were settled, I said, "That was a lot of work on letters and sounds! Let's celebrate by singing the alphabet song. Use your chart to follow along," I said as we began singing together.

"Readers, remember that you can keep your ABC chart next to you whenever you are reading. You can read it to warm up for reading your books or check it whenever you need to remember the sound a letter makes. Use it just like the big alphabet chart in our meeting area.

"Speaking of the alphabet chart, I've got a game we can play." I gestured for the children to stand, and we used a singing game to close reading workshop for the day.

> *(To the tune of London Bridge)*
> *"What's the first sound that you hear, that you hear, that you hear?*
> *What's the first sound that you hear*
> *at the beginning of pants?"* I pointed to my pants.

"/P/!" The children replied. "Pants, /p/," I responded, so that everyone got to hear the initial sound clearly.

> *"What's the first sound that you hear, that you hear, that you hear?*
> *What's the first sound that you hear*
> *at the beginning of sock?"* I touched my sock.

"/S/!" said the children all together. "Sock, /s/," I said back.

I continued with a few more verses, making a mental note to tuck the song into transitions across the day, perhaps even changing the focus to ending consonants ("What's the last sound that you hear?") in a couple weeks.

Readers Use Their Letter-Sound Knowledge to Help Them Read Unknown Words

MINILESSON

IN THIS SESSION, you'll teach children that they can use their letter-sound knowledge to solve unknown words.

CONNECTION

Ask students if they've ever been stopped in their tracks when reading by a word they can't figure out. Suggest that this is a good thing because it's a chance to use their knowledge of letters and sounds.

"Readers, has it ever happened to you that you are reading along, and all is fine and dandy. You are looking at the pictures, understanding the pattern, checking the letters. All is well, and then—whoa. Huh? What?

"You get stuck. You point underneath the word and can't say it because you don't know what the word says!

"Well, I am here to tell you that when reading isn't oh-so-easy for you, that's a good thing! Expect that there will be words that won't come easily to you. That's why you have sound power!"

Recruit the class to use pretend magnifying glasses to zoom in on a hard word, noticing and reading the letters the child wrote.

"*But* here is one tip about sound power. You can't use it from far away. No way! You have to get nose-close to the sounds. Let's say you were reading Sam's story about his dog," I said, placing the piece of writing under the document camera. "And you wanted to know what his dog had in its mouth. Let's say you were reading along fine and dandy":

I saw my BIG dog.

He had my _____ [mitten].

GETTING READY

✔ Tell children to choose a piece of almost finished writing from their writing folders and bring it to the meeting area (see Active Engagement).

✔ Return, in its entirety, to Sam's story from Session 7 and use Post-its to cover the words *mitten* and *fell*, or cover similar words in the writing you used (see Connection and Teaching).

✔ Prepare your large alphabet chart (see Teaching).

✔ Running records (see Conferring and Small-Group Work)

✔ Display the chart "With ABC Books, Readers Can . . ." (see Transition to Partner Time).

✔ Borrow a child's leveled book and select a few pages for a shared reading (see Share).

FIG. 8–1   Sam's story

"To learn what the dog is carrying, to read the word, you don't just look at the picture and think about the pattern. You *also* need to look really, really closely at the start of that word. Everyone bring a pretend magnifying glass up to your eyes and let's zoooooooom into this word" (to *mitten*, which is covered). "Okay, get your special magnifying glasses ready." I pretended to lift my own magnifying glass to my eye. As I did this, I removed the Post-it to show the word *mitten*.

"Let's say the first sound slowly, together," I said as I placed my finger under the beginning letter and looked at the picture. "Mitten!" Then I reread the sentence. I signaled to the children so that we could read the first two sentences of Sam's writing together:

> *I saw my BIG dog.*
>
> *He had my mitten.*

"Remember that when Sam works and works to hear all these sounds," and I pointed to the word *mitten*, "and to put all those letters down on the page to make a long word like this, he does it so readers like you and me can see the letters and make the sounds—and read the words!"

❖ **Name the teaching point.**

"Today I want to teach you that when words don't come easily to you as you read, don't back away. Instead, you can get close and use the beginning of the word. Then think, 'What word could this be?'"

Many of your readers will rely predominantly on the first consonant for now, but some readers may be ready to see and say more of the sounds in the word, especially as you connect to the work that they do in writing. As readers encounter an unknown word, it is efficient to say the beginning sound right away, all the while thinking about what is happening in the story. If readers can see and say sounds beyond the first letter, they will have gained even more visual information to help solve the word.

50

TEACHING

Guide children to figure out the other words in Sam's story.

"You must be *itching* to know what happened to the dog and Sam's mitten! So let's read Sam's words, and when you need to, you'll use your magnifying glasses to get close up to any tricky words."

I turned the page and revealed the middle of Sam's story (see Figure 8–1). We read together, without incident.

> *I said, NO NO NO!*

Convey how vital it is to read the words the author wrote: it impacts readers' understanding of the story.

"Oh, Sam's story is so exciting," I gushed. "I bet you can't wait to read his words to find out what happened!" I flipped to the next page in a hurry (see Figure 8–1). There was a Post-it covering one of the words on the page, and several children groaned when they saw it.

> *My mitten _____ (fell) out!*

"I know, I covered up one of Sam's most important words. But don't worry, you can still find out what happened. Get your magnifying glasses ready!"

I uncovered the word *fell*. "Get up close and use the letter at the beginning of the word. Think, 'What word could this be?' I'll put the alphabet chart on the easel in case you need it to power up. Lean in and do this work with your partner."

I listened in to the children, prompting them to say the first letter sound and to look at Sam's picture to come up with a word that could fit there.

After calling them back together, I placed one finger under the beginning of *fell*. With my pretend magnifying glass to my eye, I reported, "I heard so many of you get close up and say /f/, and then I heard some of you cheering because you thought that Sam's word could be *fell*." I nodded and grinned, confirming that the word was indeed *fell*.

"My mitten fell out!" we read together.

Make a deliberate decision during this lesson to remind children to use meaning as a resource, as well as the letter sounds. Throughout the lesson, you can say, "Think about what is happening," as you tap the picture.

While the lesson's focus is on using letter sounds, notice the notion that the purpose of reading—to make meaning—is ever-present.

ACTIVE ENGAGEMENT

Support readers to zoom in on the beginning of unknown words in their classmates' writing.

"Readers, earlier I asked you to bring a piece of your writing to the meeting area and to carefully sit on it. Take it out now.

"Now you'll get to practice reading your partner's writing! If you get stuck on a word, you can pull out your magnifying glass and get up close to the beginning of the word. Remember to ask yourself, 'What word could this be?' Hand your writing to your partner, and start reading!"

As I circulated among the children, I nudged them to be persistent when saying the beginning of tough words, to cross-check with the picture, and to check in with the writer after reading.

LINK

Reconvene and remind children of their ongoing work when facing challenges.

"Eyes on me, readers. Wow, no one here backed away when the words didn't come easily! All readers get stuck some-times, and if they do, they don't shrink back. Instead, they come up close, activating their sound power in a *bigger* way: by saying the letter sounds at the beginning of those hard words. Any time you feel stuck, remember just how powerful you are.

"Today you will start with private reading from your baggies, and then you can meet with your partners and read your alphabet books. Off you go!"

FIG. 8–2   Remind readers to attend to the initial sound when solving words.

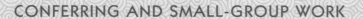

Guided Reading to Support Growth

TODAY YOUR TEACHING will presumably include the usual mix of several small groups and several one-to-one or partnership conversations. Chances are good that at least one of those small groups will be designed to help readers who are ready to move up text levels. You'll probably want to support these readers through a series of guided reading sessions.

When you look through your running records and conferring notes, you might notice a group of children reading level C books independently who are ready to receive guided reading instruction in level D texts. In addition to using meaning and structure, you have probably noticed that these readers first attend to the beginning letter and may now be starting to move their eyes across the word to attend to the final letter(s). If you look at their writing, you will probably notice that these children use and confuse

short vowels, consonant blends, and digraphs. It is likely that these children are ready for support and scaffolding in level D texts.

Before meeting with this group of children for their first guided reading session, you will want to select an appropriate level D text and plan a book introduction that is supportive, giving readers access to a more challenging text while still leaving opportunities for problem solving. Make sure you plan for how your introduction will support meaning (gist of the story or information presented, vocabulary, concept words), structure (text structure and language patterns), and visual information (tricky words).

Gather the readers together for a seven- to ten-minute guided reading session. Give the readers a book introduction, remembering that during this time children may make predictions about what will happen. You can also set them up to be reading with an eye for something specific, perhaps saying, "You'll have to read to find out if . . ." You might also want to tell youngsters, "If you finish reading before your friends, remember that you can read the book again. You might reread and make your voice sound like the character."

Distribute copies of the book to the readers, allowing each of them to read it in its entirety at their own pace. As the children are reading, coach into one reader's reading using lean prompts. For example, if you notice a reader needing support using meaning when she is word solving, you might say, "Look at all the parts of the picture before you read the words." Or "Reread and think about what would make sense." After coaching one reader briefly—for a minute—move on to the next reader.

When children have finished reading, take a little time for a comprehension check. You might ask children to check the predictions they made before reading or to look back through the pages to talk about what they learned about a topic.

(continues)

MID-WORKSHOP TEACHING
Readers Remember All Their Powers

"Readers, can I have your eyes for a minute?" I waited until I had their attention.

"I am looking around the room and see that you are really zooming in on the letters in your books. I see kids getting *nose*-close looking at letters. I saw someone looking so close at the letters that their hand was *covering* the picture!

"But hey—just because you have been working hard on your sound power, you can't forget about all your *other* powers! The picture can help you read the words too! Don't forget to pull back and also study the picture. This helps you figure out what word might make sense."

TRANSITION TO PARTNER TIME
Readers Have Many Ways to Read with Partners

"Readers, I see you all really zooming in on letters and using your sound power as you read. That got me thinking that it might be time to power up at your alphabet power stations!"

I walked to the ABC book chart. "Let's read and remember all of the fun ways to read these books together with partners." We did a shared reading of the chart together.

ANCHOR CHART

With ABC books, readers can . . .

- Ask, "Why this picture?" (Why ape for A?)
- Play "Guess What's Next!"
- Add more words.
- Sing the words!
- Play "Same and Different."

"Talk with your partners and decide how you will work with your alphabet books today. You might even invent new things to do with them!"

Many teachers end a guided reading session by giving an explicit teaching point, usually one that relates to the ways you were coaching during reading. If you coached the readers to use meaning to support word solving, you might return to a place in the text where you provided this coaching and say, "Remember that whenever you are reading and get stuck on a word, you can look closely at the picture. Then you can reread and think about what would make sense."

Take a few minutes after the guided reading session to look over your notes and decide on appropriate follow-up sessions for this group of readers. It's often wise to meet with them for a few days in a row.

Using Initial Sounds and Pictures

Reinforce using the first letters of the word and thinking about what is happening in the pictures.

"Readers, you were really zooming in closely to words, paying attention to the letters and sounds on the page! Not only were you doing that in your alphabet books, but I saw so many of you looking closely at the books in your book baggies the same way! You were checking the word, just like you check the words you write in writing workshop.

"*But* sometimes it's hard to do. Sometimes you don't know what the word is, and then you need to say the sounds and then think what the word could be. Like in Parker's book it says:

> *An elephant uses its trunk to _____.*

"If Parker doesn't know what the elephant is using the trunk for by looking at the picture, Parker can get his mouth ready to say the first sound. Watch me!" I uncovered the *w* and pursed my lips together. "I know that is the *w* and it makes the—say it with me—/w/ sound. So, what word goes with this picture that starts with the /w/ sound? Water, white, wash, whisper. What would make sense here? Wash. Let's try it."

We reread the sentence. "Yep that looks like the elephant is washing! And look, *sh* makes the /sh/ sound!

"Parker, can we borrow this book so that we can *all* practice this together, zooming in and getting our mouths ready to say the sound of the letters?"

We did a shared reading of the next page few pages of Parker's book, working together in the same way to solve and check words.

Readers Can Notice Consonant Clusters to Help Solve Unknown Words

IN THIS SESSION, you'll teach children that as books get more challenging, they will have to move from looking at just the initial consonant in a word to looking at the first two or three consonants.

GETTING READY

✓ Prepare paint, paintbrush, chocolate syrup, and milk to demonstrate blending (see Connection).

✓ Select a demonstration text, likely at level C or D. The text you use should have a pattern, picture support, and opportunities to problem-solve using the picture and consonant blends. We use *Can you see the eggs?* (pages 2–7) by Jenny Giles (see Teaching and Active Engagement).

✓ Gather white boards, dry erase markers, and erasers for the children to use during the minilesson. You will also need to have a stapler and a picture of a smiley face on hand (see Teaching and Active Engagement).

✓ Display the blends and digraphs chart (see Share).

✓ Be ready to borrow from a reader a leveled book that has a word that begins with a digraph, or chart the example we used, "I am a child," with picture support (see Share).

✓ Prepare small copies of the easy blends chart for each student's baggie (see Share).

MINILESSON

CONNECTION

Highlight that sounds can be blended together.

I called the children to the meeting area with our gathering song. "Readers, you did a lot of fun things yesterday with the alphabet. Today I'm going to show you one more really cool thing you can do with letters and sounds.

"First, let me ask you something. Have any of you ever blended two things together to make something new?" I picked up a paintbrush and made a blue streak across the page of chart paper. "Like, have you ever painted a blue sky, then blended in a bit of red or pink, and gotten a purpley color?" I added a smaller streak of pinkish red, turning part of the blue sky purple. "Or have you ever blended these colors?" I asked, and blended red and yellow. "Look what you get!"

The kids chimed in, "Orange!"

I sometimes blend things when I cook, too. Has anyone here ever taken this," and I held up chocolate syrup, "and blended it with white milk? What do you get?"

"Chocolate milk!" the kids chimed.

I nodded. "I'm telling you this because readers and writers don't just blend colors and chocolate milk. They also blend sounds."

✤ **Name the teaching point.**

"Today I want to teach you that sometimes readers can blend beginning sounds together to help them solve words. Readers can get their mouths ready for the beginning part of tricky words."

TEACHING AND ACTIVE ENGAGEMENT

Recruit kids to join you in hearing and writing the sounds at the start of some familiar words, using white boards to make this a communal activity.

"Readers, let's work with blends first as writers, and then as readers." I distributed white boards, marker pens, and erasers to some of the children. Then I asked other kids to pull in close around the white boards, to help people do some really challenging writing. "Let's say you wanted to write a story about this," I said, and pulled a stapler from a bag. "What would you write at the start of this word?"

Then I said, "Say the word really, really slowly and see if you can hear the sounds—two of them—at the start of the word." I wrote:

__apler

"What sounds do you hear? Write them on your white board. When you have written the /st/ blend, hold it high!" The children did, and I cheered. "You got it! *S-t*!" Read it! See if you can think of *more* words that begin with the *s-t* blend."

Children called out more *s-t* words, and I wrote them on the chart paper: *stone, stop, stairs.*

"I have a new blend for you," I said, and pulled out a picture of a big smile. "It is what you are making me do right now," and pointed to my upturned mouth. Then I said, "Say the word slowly and see if you can hear a blend of sounds at the start of the word! Write it on your white board!" I wrote:

__ile

Again I asked for the white boards to be held high and for kids to generate other words that start with /sm/. I had to give hints to help them think of *smart* and *smelly*.

Shift to reading, telling kids that you have chosen a book that can teach them about mother animals and their eggs and, at the same time, about blends.

"So, readers, now I want to show you a new book that we are going to be reading a lot for the next few days." I tapped the cover and read the title aloud. "It is a special book because it can teach us about mother animals and their eggs. I'll read the first few pages of the book to you, though I would *love* your help with it."

You will probably have introduced concepts such as blends and digraphs across the day during writing workshop, shared reading, word study, and shared and interactive writing before you teach this lesson. This lesson exposes children to the concepts of blends and teaches them to be on the lookout for blends in their books. It is not our intention to explicitly teach every blend.

If a large number of the children in your class are still working on letter knowledge and letter-sound relationships, you may decide to devote some additional time to alphabet books and postpone this lesson and the following one for later in the year. If your class has a solid understanding of letters and letter-sound relationships but isn't yet attending to the initial consonant, you might decide to alter this lesson so the focus is on getting their mouths ready for the beginning sound.

You may want to continue to do some of this work during writing workshop, shared reading, shared or interactive writing, or word study, giving students further practice with this concept.

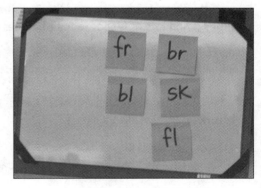

FIG. 9–1   Working with blends during word study

Mother Blackbird
is in the tree.

Her eggs are
in the nest.

Mother Fish ["Have you figured out the pattern?"]
is in the stream.

Her eggs are
in the _____ [the word stones *was covered].*

"Readers, I covered this word up because it is going to be a lot of fun to read it. Let me tell you a secret." I leaned in, cupped my hand over my mouth and whispered, "It starts with a blend!"

Mother Blackbird
is in the tree.

Her eggs are
in the nest.

2   3

Then I said to the kids, "Will *you* read this whole page to yourself in a whisper and see if you can figure out where the eggs are?" I removed the Post-it and directed them back to the start of the page.

Mother Fish
is in the stream.

Her eggs are
in the stones.

I then reconvened the children and we reread the whole page, emphasizing the word *stones*. "I thought it might be rocks at first, but the beginning blend /st/ helped us all figure out the word is *stones*.

LINK

Give readers the chance to work with just one more blend, reading one more page, and then remind them that they'll find lots of blends in their baggies of books.

"Readers, I'm only going to let you read *one more* page. This book has to last across *lots* of days, so we have to save it up. But let me tell you, this page has an animal that starts like this: /sn/.

"What animal could it be? Mother what?" As kids made the /sn/ blend sound, I tapped the picture of a snail, and soon the kids were choral reading the page.

Mother snail
is in the grass. ["Do you see the blend—/g/ /r/?"]

Her eggs are
under the ground. ["Do you see another blend—/g/ /r/?"]

If you notice readers over-relying on visual information (sound-symbol relationships), coach them to use meaning. Prompt kids to think about what is happening, how the story goes, and what would make sense. If this is a pattern in their reading behavior, you'll need to adjust your plans for the next few days to focus more on this meaning work.

I pointed to the ground and we finished reading the page.

"Readers, from this day forward, whenever you are reading, remember that sometimes just as chocolate syrup and milk can go together to make chocolate milk, two letters can go together to make a blend. Before you start reading today, see if you have any blends in your baggie of books, and if so, mark some of them so you can share them later."

FIG. 9–2 Remind readers that they can attend to blends when solving words.

Following Up with Guided Reading Groups

IN ADDITION TO ALL THE OTHER CONFERRING you will do today, it is important to make plans to follow up with the guided reading groups you met with yesterday. You can begin today's guided reading session by asking each of the students to warm up by reading the book from yesterday's session aloud to himself. As you listen to them read, you can take a quick running record on one or even on two of the readers, checking in for now at least to see which of the children can read the text you supported yesterday with 96% accuracy, fluency, and comprehension. Another time, you can analyze the running records more completely.

After a few minutes, you will want to reconvene the group and follow the structure from the previous session for introducing and reading a new text. Because the book introduction in a guided reading session is a scaffold, it is important to think about how to lighten this scaffold across the sessions. Use the information you gathered from yesterday's session and make plans to lighten the book introduction you give the group today. Think about the characteristics of this level and what the children in the group need the most support with. Include these things in your book introduction, making the decision to lighten up on some of the other things.

You should plan to work with this group (and your other groups) in one or two other sessions. One possibility for tomorrow's session might be that you gather the readers for an even lighter introduction on yet another level D book. You might give just a one- or two-sentence book introduction to the group and then let the readers preview the book with each other and get ready to read while you observe. You might prompt students by saying, "Study the first few pictures and think about how the words might go." Then as the children read, you can provide light coaching prompts as needed. Again, you'll want to try to lighten the prompts and coaching you provide to the readers. One way to do this is to use nonverbal prompts such as pointing to the picture when you want a reader to search for meaning or pointing to a small version of a chart or tool the readers are familiar with.

You can also lighten the prompts and questions you use during the comprehension check at the end of the guided reading session. During one of your follow-up sessions, you might say, "What was the book about?" rather than asking more specific questions.

It is also important to think about the ways to support these readers throughout the day. You will want to think about supporting these children during whole-class interactive read-aloud, shared reading, and interactive writing.

MID-WORKSHOP TEACHING
Celebrating Recognition of Blends

"Readers, can I have your eyes for a minute?" I waited until I had their attention.

"I see that you are really zooming in on the letters in your books. You're not just looking at the first letter in the word anymore! No way! You are zooming in on two or three and sometimes *more* letters, and blending those sounds together if you're not sure what the word is.

"Josephine was reading a little copy of our shared reading book, *My Bug Box*, and she moved her finger under the letters and blended the sounds in *twig* and *cricket*.

"I saw Isaac reading *The Itsy Bitsy Spider*, and he found blends in *spider* and *spout*. He didn't even have to blend the sounds. He just knew the blend in a snap!

"All right, readers, keep reading and keep zooming in on the blends when you come across them!"

"Readers, I'm pretty sure you know what time it is!" The children called that it was partner reading time and began restacking their books on their mats in preparation for reading them with each other.

I said, "I notice you are getting ready to read through your book stacks, and I'm glad of that. You know so many things you can do as you read with your partner! But I was thinking that today, you *might* first want to play a new reading game with your partner. This game is called 'Alphabet Pop It!'" I said, adding the activity to our partner chart.

ANCHOR CHART

Readers Read with a Partner

Decide how to read.
- ECHO, Echo, echo read.
- See-saw read.

Decide what to do.
- Add a pinch of you. (I think . . .)
- Give reminders to use POWERS!
- Hunt for snap words.
- Play "Guess What's Next!"
- **Play "Alphabet Pop It!"**

Play "Alphabet Pop It!"

"If you want to play, this is how it goes. You point to something in the picture, and then you let the first sound that word makes *pop* right out of your mouth. Then you can think about what letter or letters make that sound, and say those letters. This way you will be all warmed up if you come to those words when you are reading that page."

I held up a book that a student was reading and pointed to the picture of a store on the cover and said, "Let's let the first sounds of *store* pop right out." We all made the /st/ sound and said *s-t*. Then I pointed to the grapes in the window and said, "When I say 'Pop it,' let the first sounds in *grapes* pop right out of your mouth and then say the name of the letter or letters that make that sound. Pop it!" The class joined me in popping the sound /gr/ and saying the names of the letters. I coached students to say both the sound that the word started with and the letters the word might start with.

"You can play this game with a few of the books in your pile, and then you will probably want to go back to reading your books, as usual."

Readers Can Get Their Mouths Ready for Blends and Digraphs

Remind readers that some letters work together as a pair to make one sound (digraphs). These letters come together, but their sounds don't blend; instead they make a whole new sound.

"Readers, join me in the meeting area!" Once children had settled, I said, "I was listening in to your reading today. I heard blends at the start of many of your words! But right now, I want to show you something tricky that James came across in one of his books. Look at *this*." I put a page of a book under the document camera so that all of the children could read it:

> *I am a child.*

"At first James thought it said 'I am a boy,' because there is a boy in the picture. But then he remembered to get his mouth ready for the first part, so he tried to blend the sounds: /k/ /h/—/kh/—and it just wasn't working. The sounds didn't blend together smoothly and he couldn't think of a word that started that way and made sense there.

"Then he remembered! He remembered a story he wrote in writing workshop. He thought back to his *choice* time story, and the letters he used to write that word." I pointed to our "Choice Time" board so that the children could hear and see the word *choice* and how it was similar to the word on the page under the document camera.

"Turn and read James' page with your partner. What could that last word be?" The children quickly read the words, and then we reread the page together.

"That tricky word was *child*. The *c* and *h* come together to make a whole new sound, /ch/. So remember, some letters work together as a pair, and when you see them together they make one sound. Whenever you see *ch*, *sh*, or *th* together, you need to know and say the new sound they make together!"

Introduce the blends and digraphs chart.

I set the blends and digraphs chart on the easel. "You've been using the alphabet chart to remind you of the sounds each letter makes, and when I saw the powerful work you were doing looking at the

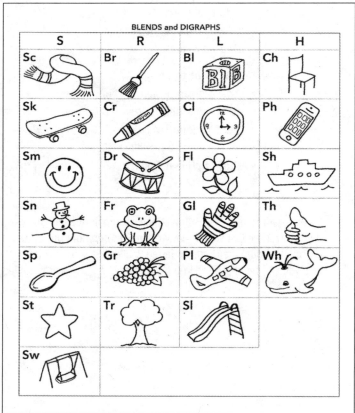

first part of words today, I realized that you might need a blended sounds chart as well. I'll give one to each of you," I said, distributing a chart to each reader. "Let's start by echo reading this." I pointed as I read and the children pointed and reread.

"Let's practice using it." I pulled out a clip from behind the easel. "Let's say the word slowly and listen for the blended sound at the beginning of the word. Does it sound like *broom* or *star* or *clock*? Point to the picture that starts like *clip*." I saw many of the students pointing to the clock.

"Listen closely as I say *clip* and *clock*. Do they start with the same blended sound?" The students agreed. "Let's look at the letters that make that blended sound." I pointed to the *cl* on the chart.

We continued practicing with pictures of a crab, a globe, and a chicken.

FIG. 9–3   Shared reading of blends chart

Readers Look to the Ends of Words as They Read

IN THIS SESSION, you'll teach children to solve words by first looking at the beginning parts of words and then moving their eyes toward the ends of the words.

GETTING READY

✓ Plan to use a dry erase board that the class can see from the meeting area (see Connection).

✓ Select a level C or D text with a repeating pattern, strong picture support, and opportunities to problem solve using the picture, the first letter or beginning part, *and* the last letter or ending part. We use pages 6–9 in *Can you see the eggs?*, by Jenny Giles. We covered grass, ground, and flower, leaving the beginning consonant blend open (see Teaching and Active Engagement).

✓ Cover the ends of several words in the text you are using. We chose to cover the words *grass* and *ground* on page 6, and *flowers* on page 8 (see Teaching and Active Engagement).

✓ Prepare a poem with Post-its masking the ending parts of words (everything after the beginning consonant/consonants). We used *We Will Go*, by Zoë Ryder White. An illustrated version is available in the online resources to print for children to add to their book baggies and reread (see Share).

✓ Ensure that you have a white board or chart paper on hand to record children's answers (see Share).

✓ Display the chart "We Are Super Readers!" (see Link). ✋

MINILESSON

CONNECTION

Tell a story about a time when you misread a word to excite the children about looking to the ends of unknown words.

As I called the children to the meeting area, I gathered them with urgency and excitement. "Boys and girls! You will not believe what happened to me this morning! While I was driving to work this morning, I passed the donut store and I saw this sign."

I wrote the words "Free Donuts" on the dry erase board. "Free Donuts! I was so excited that I drove quickly into the parking lot and ran up to the counter!" I gestured with excitement as I continued. "I ran up to the counter and I asked, 'Where are the free donuts? I'd like the free donuts!'

"I realized that everyone was looking at me like I was crazy! Then I looked down at the counter and saw the sign again, and this is what it said." I wrote the words "Fresh Donuts" on the dry erase board. "What do you notice? Zoom in and look closely." I paused dramatically and pretended to look through a magnifying glass.

Kyla called out, "It's not the same word! It says *fresh*! It says fresh donuts!"

"That's right! I'd only read the first part of the word. I was reading the word so quickly that I didn't look all the way to the end of the word! I thought that the sign said 'Free Donuts'! If I just looked a little bit further, I would have realized it had a /sh/ at the end: 'Fre*sh* Donuts'!"

❖ **Name the teaching point.**

"Today I want to teach you that when readers try to read tricky words, they need super strong *sound* power. They look closely at the beginning *and* the ending to solve the word."

TEACHING

Model reading to the end of every word.

"All right, readers, you know that as our books get more challenging, we have to zoom in and look closely at the letters the author used. When you were younger (like before the winter holiday), you solved words by just looking at the picture and getting your mouth ready with the first *sound* of the word. Then as books became more challenging, you learned how to get your mouth ready with the first *part* of the word. Now, today, I'm telling you that when words are tricky, you also need to look to the *end* of the word. Thumbs up if you are ready for the challenge." Thumbs popped up as I placed the book we started reading yesterday on the document camera and read the title before opening to page 6. Let's start by looking to the ends of the words we read yesterday.

"Oh, boy. Some words are covered! I am going to read, but when I get to that covered word, I am not going to stop at the first part. No way. I am going to look closely, all the way to the end of the word. Let's start by looking at the first part (the blend) like we did yesterday, and then you can help me look to the end."

I started reading, "Mother Snail is in the /gr/." I dragged my finger under the first two letters, and we made the sound of the first part of the word.

"That first sound gave me a clue, and when we read that word yesterday we stopped there—we didn't look to the end of this word. When I look at the picture, I can see the grass and the ground." I read the sentence with the wrong word. "Mother Snail is in the ground. That word fits. I tapped the picture. I think *grass* would also make sense. If this word is *grass*, what letter would you expect to see at the end? Grassssss," I said slowly.

"*S!*" the children called back.

"Let's check! Can you help me look closely to the end of this word to make sure you are right?" I removed the Post-it and I slid my finger under the word.

"Grass!" the kids shouted at me.

"You're right. We did it! I see the letter *s* at the end of the word, and I know that *grass* ends with /s/. It can't be ground."

Model being stuck and then rallying for the challenge.

"Okay, readers, I am going to try the next line.

"Her eggs are under the /gr/, /gr/."

I let my voice trail off and scratched my head as I stopped. I stared at the word for a moment and then back at the kids. I started to make the sound of the first letters. "/Gr/, /gr/. When I look at the picture, I can see the *gr*ound and the *gr*ass." I tapped the picture and then read the sentence with the wrong word. "Her eggs are under the grass. That word makes

While teaching this lesson, make sure that the words, as well as the picture, are visible to the kids. Even though this lesson is explicitly about using visual information, readers should always be integrating multiple sources of information. At levels C and D the picture helps to provide meaning.

Here, we stop at a word that is covered with a Post-it except for the first letters. We demonstrate that the first letters give a clue, but readers need to move their eyes to the end of the word to make sure that they read it correctly.

When children are reading level C/D books, they need to use letter-sound relationships at the beginning and end of words. We prompt readers to do this work by nudging, "Say the beginning sound and move your eyes to the ending," to solidify directionality across words. We are not yet pushing these readers to attend to the internal parts of words.

sense and it sounds right." I scratched my head again. "Should I stop there?" One of the kids told me to remove the Post-it. "That's right! I don't have to stop at the first part of the word. I can look closely to the end of the word. Do you think you can help me?" I removed the Post-it and I slid my finger under the word.

"Ground!" the kids called out.

"You're right. We did it! I see the letter *d* at the end of the word and I know that *ground* ends with /d/."

ACTIVE ENGAGEMENT

Invite students to use not only the initial but also the final letters to read a covered word.

"Readers, these books are getting harder! You will really need to look closely at the first part of the word and move your eyes to the end of the word and ask yourselves, 'Which word fits?'"

I turned the page and gestured for the students to scan the picture, before beginning to read.

Mother butterfly is on the /fl/.

"Wow! You really looked closely and got your mouth ready with the first part of the word. Now check the picture and think what might fit here, and then we will look to the end of the word. It could be flow*er* or it could be flow*ers*. They both fit.

"Put a thumb up if you think that you know what the word might be." Some of the kids popped up their thumbs. "Okay, I'll uncover it so you can read it and see if you're right!" I removed the Post-it and pointed from the beginning of the sentence as the kids read.

"Mother Butterfly is on the flower." I pointed to the last letter of the word. "The word ends with the letter *r* and I can hear the /r/ sound at the end of the word *flower*. You really looked closely all the way to the end of the word!" The children joined me in pretending to put a magnifying glass up to our eyes.

We continued the process on the next line with the word *leaf*, this time leaving the word uncovered.

Notice that you left this word uncovered. Covering the word is a scaffold that readers won't have when they are reading their books independently. So it is important to plan for at least one place for this scaffold to be released.

LINK

Remind readers to use all of their strategies as they read.

I stood by the super powers chart and pointed. "Readers, we are really powering up our sound power! We are looking at the beginning of words and moving our eyes to the letters at the end of words. But we can't forget our other powers! Let's warm up to read by reading our 'We Are Super Readers!' chart today."

FIG. 10–1 Remind readers to move their eyes to the letters at the end of the word when solving words.

Continuing to Support Children Reading Higher-Level Books

IN ADDITION TO THE CONFERRING YOU DO TODAY, you will most likely want to plan for one or two guided reading groups, perhaps encouraging a group you have worked with for a few days in a row to now work with more independence.

As you work with your readers you will want to watch for patterns in their miscues. Keep an eye out for children who tend to only check the letters as their go-to strategy and coach them also to use context clues (meaning) and their knowledge of oral language, thinking about what might sound right (structure) when problem solving. Also, watch out for kids who don't use visual information—kids who easily substitute words that make sense but who aren't looking closely enough at the print to realize that the words they are saying are not actually the words on the page. Coach these kids to look more closely as they read. Reading aloud to a partner can be especially helpful for kids who find it difficult to attend closely to the print. Rereading is also a powerful tool for supporting students with self-correcting. You can introduce several authentic, engaging reasons to reread: first of all, to rehearse for reading or talking about books with a group or a partner, and also to combine rereading with teaching students to look more closely as they read to check their words.

You'll want to continue to support your readers who are well above the benchmark, reading at levels G, H, I, or J. Check in with these readers, paying careful attention to how their reading sounds. Ensure that they are reading fluently, in meaningful phrases, and with expression. Keep in mind that if their reading is not fluent, it may interfere with comprehension.

MID-WORKSHOP TEACHING
When Readers Look to the End of a Word, They Remember What They Learned about Digraphs

I walked to the center of the room and called to the class. "Readers, can I stop you for a minute?" I waited until I had all eyes on me. "Thumbs up if you have been moving your eyes to the ends of tricky words today." I waited to see how many students had been doing this work.

"I want to remind you that some letters work together as a pair, and when you see them together they make one sound." I pointed to the blends and digraphs chart on the easel. "Whenever you see *ch*, *sh*, or *th* together, you need to know and say the new sound they make together, even when they are at the end of a word."

"I was just reading with someone who was checking to see if the word on the page was *chair* or *couch*. She saw both of those things in the picture. She knew that if the word was *chair*, she would see an *r* at the end, and if the word was *couch*, there would be a *ch*. You can always check our chart if you can't remember those sounds.

"Keep reading! Keep looking closely at those endings!"

TRANSITION TO PARTNER TIME
Partners Listen and Coach Each Other as They Read

"Readers, as your books become more and more challenging, you will need your partner *more* than *ever*! As you are reading through your books today, remember to listen closely to your partners as they read. You can look closely at the pictures and check that what they are reading makes sense. You can even keep your eyes on the words as they read and look closely, even to the ends of words as they read. If they make an oops, you can lean in and help them. You can work together, using *all* of your reading powers as you read."

You'll likely need to emphasize deeper comprehension work with these readers, because the books they are now reading will require some level of inferential thinking to understand even the most basic aspects of the stories. At the same time, you'll need to teach this higher-level thinking in a way that is accessible to very young children. To support inference work, you might begin by letting kids in on a "reading secret"—that sometimes the words and the pictures don't show the whole story. Sometimes you have to just figure it out yourself! Of course, this seems very obvious, and not secret at all, to most adults, but to a kindergartner this information is a game-changer. *Sometimes the words and the pictures don't show the whole story.* You might find a page or two where the picture and the words clearly do not show everything that happened to share as an example for teaching. "What happened in between these pages? What would make sense? Use what you know about the characters and what is happening to make a good guess." That's inference.

Guess the Covered Word

Introduce a new game called "Guess the Covered Word," an adaptation of an activity by Patricia Cunningham, to help readers orchestrate sources of information and read to the end of a word.

I called the students back to the meeting area, where I had a poem displayed on the easel. In the poem, the last part of each word was covered with a Post-it, while the first part remained uncovered.

In my best game announcer voice I said, "Ladies and gentlemen, get ready to play . . . 'Guess the Covered Word'!" The children cheered.

"Here are the rules," I continued in the voice of an announcer. "When you get to a covered word, you will first get your mouth ready with the first sound and think, 'What would make sense and sound right in the sentence?' Then, you will make some guesses, and I will write them down. Afterward, we will uncover the rest of the word so you can look all the way to the *end* of the word and check your guesses."

I introduced the poem. "This poem is called, 'We Will Go,' by Zoë Ryder White. It is about children who all go to the circus and how they get there."

> We Will Go
>
> We will go by bike.
> We will go by train.
> We will go by taxi.
> We will go in the rain.
>
> We will go by foot.
> We will go by bus.
> We will go in the sunshine.
> The circus waits for us.

I turned to the poem as I stated, "Now let's get ready to play . . . 'Guess the Covered Word'!"

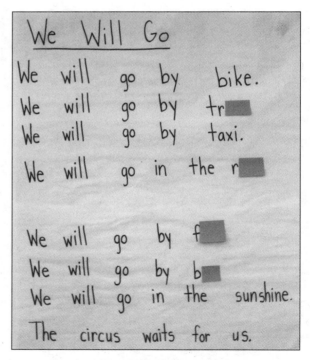

FIG. 10–2 Shared reading of "We Will Go"

I pointed under the words as we read chorally.

"We will go by bike.

We will go by /tr/"

"Ladies and gentleman, guess the covered word!"

I recorded the children's responses as they turned to talk with one another. "Okay, ladies and gentlemen, let's check if these guesses—*truck* and *train* and *tree*—make sense and start with the /tr/ sound." I pointed to the word *truck*. "Truck starts with the /tr/ sound and it could make sense that you could go somewhere by truck." I pointed to the next word. "Train also starts with /tr/ and it could make sense that you could go by train to get somewhere." I pointed to the word *tree* and rubbed my chin. "Turn and tell your partner if the word *tree* could fit here." They all agreed that *tree* did start with /tr/ but did not make sense or sound right in the context of the sentence.

"Ladies and gentlemen, what letter do you expect to find at the *end* of the word?" I paused, giving the children a moment to think. I uncovered the word *train*. The children shouted out the word *train*. "How do you know?" I asked. One of the children explained that *train* ended with the /n/ sound and that the last letter was the letter *n*.

We continued the game with the words *rain*, *foot*, and *bus* before rereading the whole poem together.

To close the workshop, I gave each student an illustrated copy of the poem to keep in their book baggies, making a mental note to continue to use an illustrated version of the poem across the week as a warm-up in shared reading.

We Will Go

We will go by bike.

We will go by train.

We will go by taxi.

We will go in the rain.

We will go by foot.

We will go by bus.

We will go in the sunshine.

The circus waits for us!

By Zoë Ryder White
Illustrated by Ramon Hamilton

Readers Preview a Page and Locate Known Words before Reading

IN THIS SESSION, you'll teach children that they can locate known words and read these words in a snap.

GETTING READY

✔ Select a level C or D text with familiar high-frequency words to display to the class. We use *Can you see the eggs?* (pages 2–9), by Jenny Giles. You may use a big book or place a book under the document camera (see Teaching and Active Engagement).

✔ Have dry erase boards and markers on hand (see Conferring and Small-Group Work).

✔ High-frequency words assessment (see Conferring and Small-Group Work)

✔ Display your chart "Readers Read with a Partner" (see Transition to Partner Time).

✔ Ensure that students have snap words on a ring in their book baggies (see Transition to Partner Time).

✔ Gather magnetic letters to use for breaking words with endings. We use the familiar words *likes* and *sees*. You may choose other familiar high-frequency words that appear often in level B and C texts, such as *comes*, *looks*, or *plays* (see Conferring and Small-Group Work and Share).

✔ Plan to read the class book "We Like to Read!" that was created during Sessions 2 and 4 (see Share).

MINILESSON

CONNECTION

Remind readers that when they know a word, they shouldn't slow down to solve it. They should read it in a snap.

"Readers, I was thinking about how each of you has been zooming in to look closely and use what you know about letters and sounds to help you solve words. When you get to a word you aren't sure about, you *slow* down, look at the picture, and get your mouth ready for the first letters. And the *cool* thing is that you do the same thing during writing time. When you get to a word you aren't sure about, you stop, say the word *slowly*, and listen for sounds you hear.

"But you know what? In writing you know that you don't always have to *slow* down. When you just know a word like that," and I snapped my fingers, "you write it in a snap. Right? It is the exact same thing when you are reading. Any book in the whole wide world will have tons and tons of snap words. More than half the words in any one of the books on our shelves are snap words. Honest!"

❖ **Name the teaching point.**

"So today I want to remind you that *yes*, when reading *some* words (words that aren't snap words), readers bring out their magnifying glasses and look closely at the letters. But when they come to a snap word, they put the magnifying glass away! They don't need to slow down or read closely. They just look at the word and they know it in a snap."

TEACHING

Demonstrate for children how scanning the pages of a book to locate known words can help them read the book and read words they know in a snap.

"So let's continue reading that great book *Can you see the eggs?*, the one about the mother animals and the eggs. To read more of that book, we will definitely need to have our magnifying glasses on hand and ready to go. We know there will be parts where we will *slow* down and look closely to read some of the words.

"*But* will we read every word *slowly*, with our magnifying glasses on hand? No way! Remember that every book in the world is brim full of words that you and I know and can say in a snap.

"So let's reread the pages we already read in this book, noticing the snap words and letting them help us read along so our reading sounds smooth. Then we can read another page or two of our book, and to do that, we'll have to shift between zooming in," and I gestured to show a magnifying glass, "and reading in a snap," and I snapped my fingers. I opened the book to page 2. I first used my finger to search the picture, and then said to myself, "Let me just look over this page and see if there are some snap words." With kids helping, I found a bunch of them. "Okay, I'm ready to read. Will you help?" I asked the kids, and brought out my pointer. The kids read with me:

> *Mother Blackbird*
> *is in the tree.*
>
> *Her eggs are*
> *in the nest.*

After we finished reading the page, I let out a sigh and exclaimed, "Wow! When we found the words we already knew in a snap, it helped us read most of the words on this page, didn't it? Will you reread the page?" We reread, and then I said, "Did you *see* all those snap words? Holy moly." I pointed under them, and we read on.

> *Mother Fish*
> *is in the stream.*
>
> *Her eggs are*
> *in the stones.*

Recap the work you just did with the class and provide another opportunity for practice.

"Wow! When you knew a word, you didn't *slow* down. No way! You just read it in a snap." And when you got to those blends, you had no trouble! Good going." We read on:

> *Mother Snail*
> *is in the grass.*
>
> *Her eggs are*
> *under the ground.*

Notice the connection to writing fluency being used as an entry point to support fluency in reading. You should reinforce this fluency work when listening to children read by expecting and complimenting instant recognition of known high-frequency words. You'll also want to make it clear that when children slow down to solve an unknown word, after solving it, they have to speed up again.

Notice the many ways the children are engaged in the reading work during the teaching portion of this minilesson: being prompted to think alongside the teacher and reread. It is also important to notice that these teaching moves don't disrupt the pacing or flow of the minilesson.

ACTIVE ENGAGEMENT

Channel readers to continue without support from you, with partners reading the upcoming text to each other.

"Work with your partner to figure out the next page on your own, if you can," I began, "but let's remember to first get ready to read the page." I moved my finger around the picture and then pointed under a few of the high-frequency words that dotted the page. "Try it," I continued, and watched while children helped each other to read some of the words in a snap and to pull in and work with the picture, pattern, and some of the letters to read other words.

Recap the reading work the children did in a way that is transferable to other books on other days.

After a moment, I stopped the children. "Thumbs up if you found a lot of words you know." Thumbs popped up in the air. "Wow! Knowing a lot of snap words helped you read the pages in this book, and it is going to help you read most of the words in lots of books."

LINK

Remind children that they can read the word wall (or their word ring) as a warm-up before reading their books and, for fun, can take on different voices to read the words.

I gestured to the word wall as I said, "I think right now would be a good time to celebrate all the snap words you know!" The children nodded in agreement. "Let's get warmed up for reading time by reading our word wall together and changing our voices when we do it. Let's read it with a mad voice. Go ahead and stand up." Everyone stood up. I started pointing to the words on the word wall, and the children chimed in, reading along with their best mad voices and faces (some of them making fists with their hands and stomping their feet).

"Wow! You really do know a lot of snap words. Remember that you can always get snap word power ready by reading the word wall before you read your books."

"Can we read it with *funny* voices?" Keegan blurted out.

"Absolutely!" I acknowledged, and we tried that.

"Now, as you go off to read, remember to watch out for these words in your books and make sure to read them in a snap!"

Even though the focus of this lesson is on reading known words in text with automaticity, you will still search for meaning instead of going directly to the print. This is a deliberate decision. When readers are reading independently or with a partner, you want them to be in the habit of searching the picture for meaning before going to the print. Remember that children reading level C and D books should use some of the letters in a word along with meaning and structure when solving unknown words.

Supporting Snap Words and Comprehension

AS YOU WORK WITH CHILDREN TODAY, both in small groups and one-on-one, you will almost surely find that a few of them need support remembering words that you thought they had already learned. When you see this, remember first that children develop this way. They learn, unlearn, and relearn, all the time, and therefore need repeated practice. It is, on the other hand, important that you provide that repeated practice because one of the most important ways that children progress as readers at this point is by becoming familiar with more words.

You can identify kids who aren't remembering previously-learned words by noticing when they can read a snap word in one text but not in another. Alternatively, you can refer to the high-frequency words assessment data you have collected. If you are teaching this unit in January/February of kindergarten, children should, at this point in the year, be developing a greater bank of high-frequency words (approximately reading between twelve and twenty words). Pull the children who are below this benchmark together for small-group work.

Start your small group by placing a model of a word on the board. Using magnetic letters, build the word left to right, slide your finger under the word, and read it to the children. Have them read the word. Then, pass each child her own magnetic letters (one by one) to build the word from left to right. Have them slide a finger under the word as they read it out loud. Let the child do this repeatedly. Eventually, remove your model and have them build the word again. To increase the challenge, jumble the letters and ask children to re-create the word.

When a child is reading a story and comes to a word that you thought would be familiar to her, pull out a small dry erase board and say to the child, "This is a word you will see often. It's ___. Let's write it." Then you can ask her to write the word several times. Scaffold this activity by first providing a model of the word on the dry erase board for the child to copy and by gradually having the child write the word without the model. Be careful not to overload children by working on too many words during a session. You may need to work on one or two words for several days, depending on the child's progress.

(continues)

MID-WORKSHOP TEACHING
Read Your Snap Word Ring as a Celebration

"Readers, can I have your eyes and ears?" I waited a moment until I had the attention of the class and dramatically raised Emanuel's snap word ring into the air.

"Each one of you has so much snap word power, and I just can't believe how much this power keeps *growing* and *growing* (just like you)! Just look at how many snap words each of you has on your snap word ring. Wow-zer! Remember that you can always build up your snap word power by rereading your snap word ring. When you finish a book, you can celebrate by rereading your snap word ring."

TRANSITION TO PARTNER TIME Partners Can Hunt for Snap Words and Turn More Words into Snap Words

"Readers, it's partner reading time." The students turned hip to hip and began restacking their books on their mats in preparation for reading with each other. I said, "I notice that you are getting ready to read through your book stacks. I want to remind you and your partner that you always warm up with a snap word hunt before you read a book with your partner."

Some kids may benefit from writing an enlarged version of the word on the board, and even from tracing those letters afterward. The point of this is to engage the child in whole-body work with the word, so the size matters. You can also ask the child to close his eyes and "see" the word in his brain or to "take a picture of it" with an imaginary camera. Remind him that later today and tomorrow, you hope he can still see that word. "Fix it in your brain."

It can help to write the words a child knows, plus one or two partially known words, on index cards (one word per card) and to keep those words on a ring or stored in a little box. Every reading workshop, the child might review the word ring as a warm-up. This helps the child build a bank of known words to use when reading. Encourage the child to use the word ring and other tools during writing as well as reading. Marie Clay recommends, "One way of remembering a word in all its detail is to be able to write it" (*Literacy Lessons Designed for Individuals*, Part Two, Marie Clay, 2005).

Although you will want to support print strategies, you also need to attend to comprehension. One way to do this is to notice whether partners talk about their books—and to be sure they do. If you notice partners reading one book, then another, then another without talking about their books, you can use this as a time to remind them that readers don't just *read* books together. They also *talk about* their books. Remember that in the previous units, children were taught to talk about "wow" pages and funny and favorite parts of books. Reinforce that when readers finish one book, they can think about a part or parts they want to talk about, perhaps marking them with Post-its. You could also support comprehension by reminding these readers that they can use the last page or part to discuss what the book was about before reading another book together.

Looking to the End of Familiar Words

Work with words in isolation to help children manipulate a common word ending.

As the children gathered in the meeting area, I prepared a set of magnetic letters to make the following words: *sees* and *likes*.

"Readers, you've been trying hard to watch out for snap words and read them in a . . . snap! But you know what? Sometimes—listen to this!—snap words *hide*. You might look at a word and say, "That's *not* a snap word!" But then, if you look again, *really* closely, you'll see that the first part is a snap word! You can read the snap word, look to the end, and read the ending too!

"I am going to put up the letters from one of our snap words. As I put each letter up on the easel, say the letter's name."

"*S! E! E!*" the children called out, after I placed each one on the magnetic easel. "Now read the word," I said, as I ran my finger under the word. When the children responded, "See!" I nodded my head and snapped my fingers. "You did know that word in a snap!

"Like I said before, sometimes we put endings on our words. What's this ending?" I held up an *s* and the children named the letter in unison. "Watch this!" I leaned toward the children and with an exaggerated motion I placed the letter at the end of *see* to make the word *sees*. "When we break this word, we go *see*," and I slid the whole word to the left, "/ ssss/." I slid the *s* to join the rest of the word. "*Sees*," I read, as I ran my finger under the word. To reinforce one-to-one matching, I pointed crisply under the word and reread it aloud.

Next, I called a reader who, based on running records, needed support with high-frequency word recognition. "Zach, you break the word. Readers, as Zach breaks the word, say the parts with him. Stand in a way that lets everyone see when you slide your finger!" I was careful to repeat just what I had modeled before, and coached Zach as he moved the word *see* to the left, followed by the *s* and read it while running his finger underneath. "Now point under it," I whispered to Zach, leading the class to reread *sees*.

Move your word work into the context of a familiar text.

I repeated the process with the word *likes*, and then moved it out of isolation and into context. "Readers, let's find that word in our class book 'We Like to Read!'" I held up our book and we read the title together. Once I turned to the first page, I whispered to the children, "Do you see a snap word hiding here? Thumbs up when you do!"

Eagerly, the children raised their thumbs and we reread the page all together. After rereading the whole book, stopping to locate the word *likes*, I reminded readers, "Remember, you know your snap words, even when they have endings!"

Readers Check Their Reading

MINILESSON

CONNECTION

Celebrate how children work hard to check their *writing* so it is easy for readers to read. Compare this to the work that readers do after they solve words.

As we sang our gathering song, the children assembled in the meeting area, and then I began. "Readers, you have been working so hard to use your sound power and snap word power. It is really helping you read so many new books! When I was thinking about how high you have turned these powers up, I realized something even more *amazing*: you don't only use these powers in reading. You also use them in writing."

"Thumbs up if you remember fixing and fancying up your writing for our last writing celebration—the celebration when everyone had a special guest join us." Thumbs shot up in the air.

"When we were getting ready for that *very* special writing celebration, you worked by yourself and with your writing partner to check your writing and make it easier to read. You really zoomed in and looked closely, working so hard to make sure that your writing made sense, sounded like a book, *and* looked right. Do you remember that?" The children nodded in agreement.

I gestured toward the "Check Your Reading!" chart as I said, "You are already the kind of readers who always *check* your reading to make sure that it makes sense," I touched my head, "and sounds like a book," I touched my ear. "And just like writers do, readers also zoom in and make sure their reading looks right." As I said "looks right" I pointed to the new part of the chart and tapped my pointer finger beside my eye.

IN THIS SESSION, you'll teach children that even after they think they have solved words, their reading work is not finished. You will show the class that readers monitor for meaning, structure, and visual information. If their reading doesn't make sense, sound right, or look right, they must fix it up.

GETTING READY

✔ Display the chart "Check Your Reading!" that was created in Session 5 of this unit. Ahead of time, add 'Does it look right?' to this chart (see Connection).

✔ Prepare places to make miscues in a level C or D book. Plan to miscue in a way that doesn't take visual information into account. You will want to cover one word for the teaching and one word for the active engagement to help children use meaning and structure with visual information. We use *Can you see the eggs?*, by Jenny Giles, and chose to cover the words *sand* on page 10 and *pond* on page 12 (see Teaching and Active Engagement).

✔ Display the chart "We Are Super Readers!" (see Link and Transition to Partner Time).

✔ Gather up counters, quarters, or similar objects and prepare Elkonin boxes to use when working with small groups (see Conferring and Small-Group Work).

✔ Select a familiar text to use for rereading. We use *Can you see the eggs?*, by Jenny Giles (see Share).

✔ Prepare a celebratory song on chart paper. We use "We Have Sound Power" (see Share).

✤ **Name the teaching point.**

"Today I want to teach you that just like *writers* check over their writing, so, too, *readers* check over their reading. After readers work hard to read the words on a page, they stop and ask, "Does it make sense? Does it sound right? Does it look right? If things seem off, readers reread to fix it up."

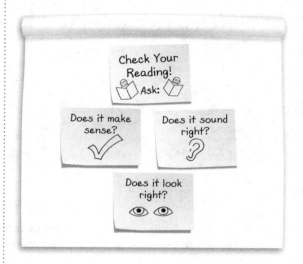

TEACHING

Demonstrate how you check your reading and fix up parts that don't make sense, sound right, or look right.

"When I read this book, I am going to be the kind of reader who works *really* hard to read the words on every page *and* checks my reading."

I placed *Can you see the eggs?* on the document camera. After I looked at the front cover and read the title aloud, I flipped to pages 10 and 11. "When we get to a tricky word, I am going to work hard to think about words that would fit. Make sure you give me a thumbs up if you have any ideas."

I pointed under the first word and began reading, stopping when I got to the tricky word, which was covered.

> *Mother Snake*
> *is on the _____. [sand]*

"Oh! This is a tricky word! Let me think about a word that would fit here." I tapped the picture as I said, "*Dirt* would make sense and sound right. Let's look at the word and zoom in closely to make sure it looks right."

I uncovered the word and said, "Dirt. Does that look right?" I placed my finger at the beginning, moving it across the word until I reached the end. I shook my head and let out a sigh, "*Nope*. That doesn't *look* right. I need to try something to fix my reading."

In Session 5 you used clear gestures to reinforce the monitoring cues you taught. Make sure you continue to use the same gestures you taught your class earlier in the year. Notice that you will add a clear gesture for "looks right." You will want to remember to use these gestures to help children internalize and remember the work they need to do as readers.

For visual/graphophonic miscues you will want to substitute words that make sense and sound right while ignoring sound-symbol relationships. This will allow you to model checking that a word "looks right."

Demonstrate using several strategies to correct the miscue before continuing to read.

I reread the sentence quickly, pausing when I got to the tricky word, making sure to look at the picture, talk about what I saw, and say the sound of the first letter(s). "*/S/, /s/, sand*! *Yes*, sand makes sense and sounds right here! That looks right because it starts with the letter *s*." I slid my finger under the word as I said, "I hear the */d/* at the end of the word and it ends with *d*."

I gestured to the chart as I said, "Did you see what I did? After I worked hard to read the words on the page, I made sure to check my reading. When something wasn't right, I used all my strength and powers to fix it up! Give me a thumbs up if you are that kind of reader—the kind of reader who is always checking your reading." Thumbs popped up all around.

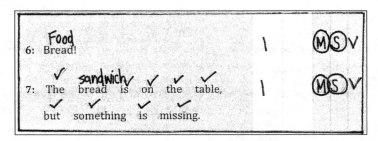

FIG. 12–1   Notice that this reader is using meaning and structure to solve the word. Today's lesson will be especially helpful for readers like this.

ACTIVE ENGAGEMENT

Channel children to check and fix their reading.

I turned to pages 12 and 13 and said, "Now it is your turn. Let's read this page together. When we get to the tricky word, we will think about words that would fit. Then we will look at the word to make sure it looks right."

I turned the page and moved my finger around the picture on page 12 before pointing under the words. The children chimed in and I paused when we got to the covered word.

> *Mother Frog*
> *is on the leaf.*
>
> *Her eggs are*
> *in the _____. [pond]*

"Let's think about some words that would make sense and sound right. Give me a thumbs up when you have some ideas." I waited until I saw thumbs in the air, and then prompted the children to share with their partner.

"Readers, you were thinking it could be *water*. That would make sense and sound right. Now, let's zoom in and look at the word closely to make sure it looks right." I uncovered the word and said, "Water. Does that look right?" I pointed to the initial consonant and moved my finger across the word.

"Pond," the children said aloud.

"Let's reread and check our reading."

We then read the next page together, making sure to stop and check our reading, before finishing the book.

You won't want to cover a word on page 14 or for the remainder of the book. Covering the word is a scaffold that readers won't have when they are reading their books independently. So it is important to plan for at least one place for this scaffold to be released.

LINK

Remind children that they are the kind of readers who work hard to read and understand their books, and they always check their reading.

"Wow! I knew you were the kind of readers who always check your reading. Remember that after you work hard to read your books, you have to stop and check your reading. If you say, "Yup. That makes sense! That sounds right—just like a book! That *looks* right! You can keep on reading."

Then I gestured to the "We Are Super Readers!" chart and said, "But remember, if something isn't quite right, remember to use all your powers and strength to fix it up."

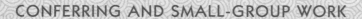
Supporting Students Who Need to Build Phonemic Awareness

AS YOU PROGRESS THROUGH THIS UNIT, you will want to continually refer back to your notes and assessments to plan for a variety of small groups and conferences.

You will want to be sure to check on which of your kids still don't have the phonemic awareness that is a major building block in a child's learning to read. Progress for these kids will be slow until you address this need. Children must be able to *hear* the sounds in words as they learn the connection between letter sounds and their visual representations. This is their sound power! You can tell which kids need support with phonemic awareness by reviewing your observation notes and assessment data. Can they demonstrate their understanding of hearing sounds in words by isolating and manipulating those sounds? Can they tell you the first sound in *man?* Can they tell you the last sound in *hug?* Can they tell you the sounds of a word in sequence? For example, if you ask, "What sounds do you hear in *cat?*" they say, "Cccaaattt." Can they put separate sounds together to form a word? For example, if you say, "Rrru-uuggg," stretching out the sounds like natural speech, can the child say, "Rug"? Can they hear and identify the same sound in different words? For example, if you were to say, "Ball, boy, bat," and ask what sound is the same in all the words, the child would identify the /b/ sound.

Consider it a priority to work with children in mid-kindergarten who do not demonstrate phonemic awareness. You will want to work with them every day in activities that emphasize the concept that words have sounds. Marie Clay found that hearing larger chunks of sound is easier for a child who has challenges hearing sounds in words (*Literacy Lessons Designed for Individuals*, Part Two, Marie Clay, 2005). Start by helping the child to hear and clap the syllables she hears in familiar two- or three-syllable words. When the child is secure in doing this, move on to stretching out the sounds in simple CVC words, such as "ccc-aaa-ttt." Ask her to look at your lips as you do this, to emphasize that it is not staccato, but smooth. Chopping words unnaturally may develop into a habit that will be hard to break.

You might also use Elkonin boxes as a visual scaffold once a child is able to say a word slowly, stretching out the sounds (not in a choppy or staccato manner). Draw a box for

(continues)

MID-WORKSHOP TEACHING
The Blends Chart Can Support Checking

"Readers, give me your eyes for just a moment. So many of you are using your magnifying glasses to zoom in to the letters in your words to check that your reading looks right! Remember a few days ago we played a game with our big blends chart?" The children nodded.

"Well, just like our ABC books, the blends chart can be a power station for readers. As you are checking that your reading looks right, you might find a blend in a word. You can notice the blend right away, instead of spending time saying the sounds of each letter! You will be able to read and check even faster! To do this, you can get to know the blends chart really well. You can read, read, read your blends, and soon enough, you'll know sounds in a *snap*, just like your snap words!

"I am so glad you have your own blends charts; keep them close by, and use them to power up when you need to! You can even warm up by reading your chart before you read your books, just like we do sometimes in shared reading and word study!"

Partners Can Help When Something Is Not Right

"It's partner time!" I said as children began restacking their books on their mats. "I notice you're getting ready to read through your book stacks with your partner, and I want to remind you that partners have important jobs to do when they are reading together. Partners need to look and listen to each other's reading with care and lean in to help when something is not right.

"As your partner is reading, listen carefully to make sure that what they are reading makes sense and sounds right. You can also have your eyes on the words as they are reading to see if their reading *looks* right. If you notice that something is not right, you can say, 'Oops!' Then lean in and help to fix it up."

each sound, not for the letter. For example, the word *cat* will have three boxes, whereas the word *toy* will have two boxes.

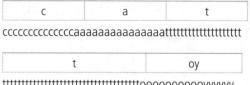

c	a	t

ccccccccccccccaaaaaaaaaaaaaaaaaatttttttttttttttttttttt

t	oy

tttttttttttttttttttttttttttttttttttttttoooooooooooyyyyyy

Use counters, quarters, or similar objects and model pushing the object into the corresponding box as you say each sound. For example, as you say the word "ccccc-aaaa-tttt," push the object into the first box as you say "cccccc," the second counter into the second box as you say "aaaaa," and the last counter in the third box as you say "tttttt." (Remember to say it slowly, as in natural speech, without isolating each individual sound.) Then run your finger from left-to-right under the boxes and say *cat*. Transfer the responsibility to the child and have him do the activity independently, with coaching as needed. You might help push the objects, slowly articulating the word for the child until he can do it on his own. Once the reader has done some of this work, you can coach him to put a letter in each box to represent the sound heard. You may want to do this work using words that are pictured in the books in the student's baggie, to help students see how these activities transfer to reading their just-right books.

Celebrate All that Readers Know about Letters and Sounds

Congratulate students on becoming stronger as readers, and participate in a shared reading.

"Wow," I admired, bringing the class together in the meeting area. "You have really been using your sound power! Let's use that power and all that we know about being a strong reader to read our book again."

I placed the text *Can you see the eggs?* under the document camera, and we began reading together. From time to time we paused to look at the beginning of a word, look across to the last letters, notice a snap word, and check our reading. After finishing the book, I gave children the opportunity to quickly tell their partner what the book was all about, emphasizing the importance of reading for meaning.

Celebrate together by singing a song.

"Before we end our reading workshop for today, I want to look at you all closely. Sit up tall so I can get a really good look." The children straightened up. Some puffed out their chests. A few partners looked at one another, smiling sheepishly, as though they knew something was different.

I leaned closer and examined them with my finger—magnifying glass to my eye. "Yes. Yes, I thought so. This is amazing. Truly amazing! You all look a little stronger. Readers, I can detect," I straightened my magnifying glass, "that with all the hard work you have done over the last few days, your sound power has grown to four times its original size! To celebrate, I wanted to sing a song *to* you, *about* you. As soon as you are ready, join me in singing to your friends."

I uncovered the words to the song and began singing. Soon the children's voices matched mine, and we sang the song a few more times as they danced along with the new words set to *The Alphabet Song*.

We have sound power
Yes we do
We have sound power
How 'bout you?

Look at the picture
Say the first sound
Move your eyes to the end
and read what you found

We have sound power
YES WE DO!
We have sound power
How 'bout you?

FIG. 12–2   Shared reading of celebration song

As Books Become Harder, Readers Need New Kinds of Picture Power

IN THIS SESSION, you'll teach children that they can graduate to new powers. These books will put new demands on them, including the need to use picture power differently.

GETTING READY

✔ Cue the song "Pomp and Circumstance" on a music player, and have pictures of people in graduation gowns ready to share (see Connection).

✔ Prepare to read the first few pages of *Oh, the Places You'll Go!*, by Dr. Seuss (see Connection).

✔ Select a familiar level A, B, or C book with a simple pattern and very strong picture support. We use *Picnic*, by Phyllis Root (see Teaching).

✔ Select a second, more challenging pattern book where the picture support is less obvious. We use *Ethan's Cat*, by Johanna Hurwitz (see Teaching and Active Engagement).

✔ Prepare the beginning of an interactive writing text titled "Our Favorite Toys!" that students can finish with you in a conference or small group (see Conferring and Small-Group Work).

✔ Prepare an extra-strength icon to add to the "We Are Super Readers!" chart (see Mid-Workshop Teaching).

✔ Record a handful of prepositions, each on a separate piece of paper, to use in a game of "Simon Says" (see Share).

✔ Prepare the poem, "My Dog," to read together (see Share).

MINILESSON

CONNECTION

Recruit students to participate in a miniature graduation march from their seats to the meeting area.

Before asking children to come to the meeting area, I said, "Readers, have any of you ever been to a graduation? Do you know what that is?" Some children had been to graduations, and they helped co-construct a shared understanding of graduations as a ceremony for people who are finishing a part of school and moving on to higher levels—to middle school, high school, or college.

"I'm asking because today is graduation day for you as readers," I said. "I'm going to play a famous graduation song while you parade around the room in a very proper way. Pretend you have caps and gowns on." I showed children a picture of traditional graduation robes as I turned on "Pomp and Circumstance" and gestured for the kids to form a processional. The children walked in procession around the circumference of the room to the meeting area, where every child stood in her spot.

Once everyone was facing me, I turned off the music and said in my most official voice, "Please be seated." Then I sat down formally in my chair, opened *Oh, the Places You'll Go!*, by Dr. Seuss, and read the first two stanzas.

Emphasize how much readers have grown in just a few short weeks and that they are now ready to use more sophisticated reading strategies.

"You are different readers now than you were when we started our unit." I paused to look into children's eyes. "You've grown so strong as readers that *now* you are ready to graduate. You are graduating to more challenging books.

"But here is the thing, your books are changing, and *you* have to change, too. Your powers need to graduate too. They need to be able to do new things. So let's start with this power right here," I said pointing to "picture power" on our chart. "Let's make our picture power *extra* strong!"

❧ Name the teaching point.

"Today I want to teach you that now that you are reading more challenging books, you can't just quick-check the picture to figure out the word. You have to use the *whole* picture to think about what you see and what's happening."

TEACHING

Display pages from a book with simple, clear pictures.

"When you read a book like this," I put up a part from *Picnic*, "you used to read the words like this."

> *Mouse finds a . . .*

"Then you looked at the picture, saw a cookie, and would then read *cookie*. It was that easy. You would just check the picture and look for one thing!"

Teach readers to use extra-strength picture power to help them read challenging books.

"But you have graduated!" I said, as I hummed a few measures of "Pomp and Circumstance." "And now it may not be as easy to read some of the books you've chosen. Most of you have books like this one, *Ethan's Cat*. In books like this, there is more to the pattern, more to the picture, and more to what is happening. You can't just check the picture for one thing. You have to use the *whole* picture and really think about what is happening. Let me show you."

Demonstrate looking at lots of details in the picture.

Placing *Ethan's Cat* under the document camera, I started to read, pausing on the second page.

> *Ethan holds a cat.*
> *Ethan chases the cat . . .*

"Okay, let me use extra-strength picture power to think about what is happening and read the last three words. Ooooh! I see that some of you already know. Here I see the cat. It looks like she is jumping over the fence here in the garden. Now let me go back and reread and see if that helps me read the words."

> *Ethan chases the cat over the fence.*

This mini graduation ceremony sets up a sequence of teaching that will help readers "graduate" to more challenging books and stronger reading powers.

For many of your readers, a new challenge will be that the illustrations in their books are now more involved, and some of the tricky words in their books might not only name objects in the picture, but also perhaps the adjectives and adverbs that describe those objects and prepositional phrases that show where they are (although you would not need to mention parts of speech to children in this moment!).

"Yep, that is three words," I said, pointing to the words. Then returning to the picture, I continued, "The cat is jumping over the fence, so it makes sense too! Do you see how I used extra-strength picture power, I didn't just say *fence*. I studied the picture and said what was happening to help me figure out the last part of the sentence.

"Let me do it again. You can do it with me."

Ethan chases the cat . . .

"Let's use our extra-strength picture power. I am going to say what I see happening. Ethan is running after the cat and the cat is trying to get away by sneaking under this bush or tree.

"Is that what you were thinking, too? Let's see what the author wrote here. I think this will help us read the long sentence."

Ethan chases the cat under a bush.

"Does that make sense? Is it three words and does it fit? Yep it does. So, do you see how there is more to the book and more that I have to do to read it? To a read a book like *this* one, you have to use the pictures more, not just look for one thing and name it!"

ACTIVE ENGAGEMENT

Encourage children to use extra-strength picture power on the next page, by saying all that is happening in the picture and using their observations to read the text on the page.

"Now it's your turn to use extra-strength picture power! Look at the whole picture, not just one word, and try to say all that is happening in the picture. Let's read together."

Ethan chases the cat . . .

"Go ahead, talk to your partners. Say what you see happening in the picture."

"A lot of you said something like 'The cat is climbing up the tree to get away from Ethan. Let's see if that helps us read the last three words. Try it with your partner. Go!"

Ethan chases the cat up the tree.

"Whoa! I heard some of you say that Ethan chases the cat up the tree. Does that make sense? Is that what happens?" The children nodded in agreement. "Yes! You are using extra-strength picture power. You didn't just say *tree*! You searched the whole picture."

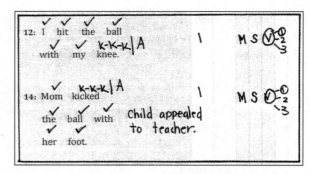

FIG. 13–1   Notice that this reader is only using visual information to attempt to solve words. Today's lesson will be especially helpful for readers like this.

In addition to searching the picture for what is happening, some books will also require children to use extra-strength picture power to help them read descriptive words: the horse is big and brown.

We finished reading the book together, practicing the strategy on the last few pages.

LINK

Make the graduating and supercharging of picture power a grand event by holding a miniature graduation ceremony.

"You might have new books in your book baggie today that feel a little challenging. You are not going to look at them and go, 'Help me! Help me! I can't! Oh, no!' No way! Instead, you'll turn up your powers! Show your reading muscles!" I turned and pointed to the super powers chart. "Are there kids in this room who would be willing to use extra-strength picture power even today, this very day?"

All the kids' hands shot up. I fell backward, slapping my forehead in mock astonishment, then sat up again quickly and began reciting the poem from the start of the minilesson as the children chimed in. For the second stanza, I substituted,

> "You have brains in your head.
> You have feet in your shoes.
>
> Get to your baggies.
> Read any book you choose!"

Using Interactive Writing to Support Reading and Supporting Stronger Readers

AFTER SOME QUICK INDIVIDUAL AND TABLE CONFERENCES to get the new bend up and going and to support readers with new books, you will want to work with small groups reading above and below benchmark. While we describe some options for small-group work, keep in mind that at least one of your groups today will likely be a guided reading group.

Chances are you have readers who needed support reading level A and B texts earlier in the unit and who, based on your running records and conferring notes, can now read level B texts independently and are ready for instruction in level C books. Because you don't want these students to linger in level B texts, make plans to support them in level C texts through a series of small-group sessions. You might work with these kids today in small-group interactive writing.

When planning for the group, think about the characteristics of texts at these readers' instructional level. Ahead of time, you can start writing what will become a shared text with the characteristics of level C texts. It might contain a complex pattern, longer sentences, and more than two lines of print on each page (i.e., Look at Keegan / with his car. / His car is little and red.).

One option is to spotlight children from the small group in this book. You could write about each child and her favorite toy and title the book "Our Favorite Toys!" You could say to the group, "Today you are going to help me finish writing a book that I started

MID-WORKSHOP TEACHING
Using Extra-Strength Picture Power

I stood at the "We Are Super Readers!" chart. "Readers, how is your extra-strength picture power? Has it helped you read your books? When you look at the whole picture and think about what is happening, you really do turn up the power!" I said, adding an extra-strength icon to the chart. "This special star will remind us that we have extra strength!"

EXTRA STRENGTH!

"Right now, find a page that made you do a lot of thinking work and put your thumb on that page. Now, reread that page, and this time, use all your extra-strength picture power to get a lot of thoughts out of the picture. I'll ask you some questions to help you do this," I said.

"Did anyone's picture tell *where* something was?" I asked, and when a few kids volunteered yes, we looked at some of their pages. One had a picture with an insect going inside a hole and another insect crawling under a leaf. I went on to ask if there were pictures that told *what* someone was doing, and *how* someone did things, each time stopping to share an example.

TRANSITION TO PARTNER TIME
Bringing Pictures to Life by Acting Them Out

"Readers—or maybe I should start calling you graduates!—can I have your eyes and ears for a minute?" I waited, and then, gesturing to the chart, I said, "It's partner reading time. Since you all have extra-strength picture power now, I'm thinking that partners might have enough combined strength to read pages by acting them out. If you are reading along and whoops!, you get stuck, you might try, as partners, to go back and act out the book, and especially the tricky part. Using your extra-strength picture power and acting out a tricky part of the story can help you figure out tricky words."

writing for each of you. After we finish it, I'll give each of you a copy for your book baggie." Then hold the book up and say, "This is a book about you and your favorite toys from our classroom. Let's read the title and the first two pages together. Then you can help me write the other pages." You could then work with the group to construct a few pages. Write some of the words that are beyond the grasp of the group members, sharing the pen for initial and final consonants and blends, the child's name, sight words, and so forth.

You'll also want to follow up with your strongest readers. If you have a handful of kids reading at very high levels (G–J) and if these students are making basic inferences about story events and character actions, you could up the ante by teaching them to notice what characters say and do to figure out not only what is happening, but also how characters feel at each part of the story. Books at these transitional levels usually feature just one or two main characters who are fairly easy to figure out (Biscuit, Puppy Mudge, Fly Guy, and Henry and Mudge are examples). Kids might role-play the part of one character, talking about how the character feels and speculating why. Or they might put a Post-it or a special bookmark in places where the character has a strong feeling (as they may have done when they read emergent storybooks earlier in the year).

Boost Vocabulary around Prepositions to Support Reading More Complex Texts

Introduce prepositions by playing Simon Says.

"Graduates," I said, when the children had gathered, "you *used to* expect pictures to be of one thing, like a ball or a bat, or a bike, and the picture would go with the one word that was tricky to read. You'd think, 'What does this say?' Then you'd look at the picture of a bike and say, 'Bike! Done.'

"But now that you have graduated and have extra-strength picture power, many of you are noticing not just what is in the picture, but *where* it is. That's wise of you! So many books work this way. Authors use a lot of different kinds of words to say where something is. It can be hard to know all of them. So I have a plan to help. I thought today we could play Simon Says to learn some words that tell *where* something is. Do you know how to play?" The children chimed yes.

"Okay! Everyone stand up! Remember, when you are 'out,' you will take a seat on the rug." As the class stood, I said, "Simon says wave your hands *above* your head." I held up a sign with the word *above*. The kids looked around at each other and followed the direction. "Simon says put your hands *behind* your back." Again, I held up a matching sign. "Lift your leg and clap your hands *under* your knee."

"You didn't say Simon Says!" shouted Isaac. I smiled, asking the kids who followed my direction to sit down.

We continued playing, with more prepositions: *around*, *between*, *beside*, *below*, *near*, *through*.

"You are pros at this! Now see if you can read my poem," I said, displaying the illustrated poem.

> *My Dog*
>
> *My dog is <u>near</u> me.*
>
> *My dog is <u>behind</u> me.*
>
> *My dog is <u>under</u> me.*
>
> *My dog is <u>ON</u> me!*

"When you are reading, my graduates, there are lots of things to be thinking about to help you read more and learn more from your books! Having new powers makes you a more powerful reader and makes reading even more fun!"

FIG. 13–2 "My Dog" poem

Session 14

Supporting Readers Who Are Moving from Pattern Books to Stories, and Bolstering Partnerships

MINILESSON

CONNECTION

Support the graduation theme by telling a story about a little kid who "read" books by memory. Point out that as books become more challenging, this is definitely not possible.

"Readers, I want to tell you a story. I once was working with a little kid—he was as old as you were way back at the start of kindergarten—and he said to me, 'Guess what? I can read with my eyes closed.'

"I knew that was impossible. You have to see the pictures and the letters to read! But then that little kid went through his baggie of books and I think he squinted just enough to see the cover of a book to know which one he was holding, because it sounded like he really *could* read those books in his baggie with his eyes closed. One went like this:

> I like red.
>
> I like green.
>
> I like blue.

"Another went:

> Monkey draws a dog.
>
> Monkey draws a bear.
>
> Monkey draws a horse.

"And there were a whole bunch of other books in that kid's book baggie. He pretended to read them all to me, and he did it with his eyes *closed!*

IN THIS SESSION, you'll teach children that some of their books might be less patterned. This means they need to rely even more on searching for meaning and on their knowledge of high-frequency words.

GETTING READY

✔ Choose a familiar text that is at or above the current benchmark and that does not have strong pattern support. You will use this book to demonstrate ways readers can strengthen snap word power. The book you select should be more of a story and not a list book. We use *Wake up, Dad*, by Beverley Randell, but this text is interchangeable with others (see Teaching, Active Engagement, and Share).

✔ Prepare an extra-strength icon to add to your "We Are Super Readers!" chart (see Link).

✔ Prepare to add a word to your word wall (see Share).

"So, readers, how did he do it?"

The kids called back that the books were patterned, and he knew the patterns. I nodded.

"But, readers, here's the important thing for you to know. You have graduated. And the books that you'll be reading as you get older and older aren't books that can be read like this," and I closed my eyes tight.

"I need to tell you something. As you get older, the patterns that helped you read are going to fall away just like training wheels on a bike eventually come off. And you are going to need stronger powers to read these new books."

✤ Name the teaching point.

"Today I want to teach you that sometimes you will be reading and *bam*, the pattern will be gone. Don't worry. You can use your extra-strength picture power and turn up your snap word power to help you."

TEACHING

Rally the class around reading more challenging texts by relying heavily on high-frequency words.

"Let's use all our powers to read a new book that is a little bit harder than the ones we're used to. Do you think reading with our eyes closed will work? No! Of course not! Our super powers won't work if our eyes our closed. We will need our eyes wide open to see the pictures and find the snap words!"

Quickly introduce the book you will use in the lesson.

As I placed a book on the document camera, I said, "This book is called *Wake up, Dad*. It is a story about three kids: Kate, Nick, and James." I pointed to the children on the cover as I said their names. "They are trying to get Dad out of bed."

I opened the book to the first page, touched parts of the picture, then read the words, pointing under them.

> *Kate is up.*
>
> *Nick is up.*
>
> *James is up.*

"Hey, this book has a pattern! I'm feeling pretty good about this!"

On the next page, I again pointed to the picture, musing to myself about the story, and then began to read, confident that this page would follow the pattern, pointing to the words.

In levels C and D, a pattern shift can happen once or several times across the book. This shift can occur within the story as well as at the end of the book. These books are more apt to tell about actions or things that are happening. The characters do something. This causes changes in the sentence structure of the books; the sentences become more complex. They are longer and can include prepositional phrases.

Dad is asleep.

I looked up at the class and said, "Maybe this is a tricky see-saw pattern book."

Dramatize being worried that the text does not have pattern support and then rising to the challenge.

I turned the page to reveal a lot more text. Then I paused, furrowing my brow, pretending to be worried. Hamming this up, I said, "Huh? This part is different! No pattern?! What will I do?"

Then, with urging from the kids, I said, "Wait, I know I can do this! First, I'll look at the picture to get ready to read the words." I pointed to the picture and thought aloud about what was happening. "I see Dad is asleep in the bed and Kate is pulling on the covers. Give a quick thumbs up if you were noticing that, too."

Channel students to help you scan the page and recognize snap words.

"Now, let's use our snap word power! Let's see if we can find any words we already know. Look closely for snap words. Thumbs up when you see some. Ooh! I see one! Oh! I see another one! I see a few!" I waited for the students to scan the page and recognize the snap words, *up*, *Dad*, *I*, and *am*. "Okay, now I'm ready to read the page and think about what is happening."

> Kate said,
>
> "Wake up, Dad."
>
> "I am asleep," said Dad.

"The pattern is *gone*, but you have snap word power to help you read the words!"

ACTIVE ENGAGEMENT

Guide children to use snap word power on the next two pages, gradually releasing your support.

"Let's keep going, and keep your eyes open!" I turned the page. "Use your extra-strength picture power first." I had the students turn and talk about the picture briefly as I voiced over, "What's happening in the picture?" "What are the people doing?" "What might they be saying?

"Now, use your snap word power and read the words. I see the word *said*." I pointed to the word. "I can read that in a snap! Thumbs up if you see more snap words on the rest of the page." I waited for kids to scan and respond. "You are snap word machines! You can do this! Remember also to think about what is happening."

I pointed, reading aloud the first line while the kids chimed in. I let my voice trail off as I pointed to the start of the second line:

While children are reading level C/D books, it will be helpful for them to learn additional high-frequency words. Students will need to continue to build up their high-frequency word bank to help them read with more automaticity. Be sure to support students with this throughout the day, especially in context.

James said,

"Wake up Dad."

"I am asleep," said Dad.

I turned to the next page. "Eeek! No pattern! Should we give up?" I nudged.

"No!" the children called back.

"That's right! You can say . . ."

"I can do this!" the kids filled in. I had the children look at the picture and search for snap words before reading the next page aloud together.

"Dad, Dad, wake up!"

said Nick.

"Wake up, Dad!

LINK

Send children off to read, reminding them to use their powers when books are not heavily patterned.

"Phew—that was hard work! You couldn't read *that* with your eyes closed!" I wiped my brow. "As books get harder, they start to change, and *you* will have to change to read them. Just like the training wheels come off your bike, the patterns will come off your books. You don't need to worry! You can use extra-strength picture power and snap word power to help you!"

Before sending the children off to read, I added an extra-strength icon next to snap word power on the chart.

EXTRA
STRENGTH!

Supporting Readers Who Are Moving from Pattern Books to Stories, and Bolstering Partnerships

EARLY ON IN THE BEND, you will want to continue to offer conferences and small groups that support children's work in new books.

Today you may decide to gather a group of children who are moving out of heavily-patterned texts to point out that many patterned books are lists. You could show them some examples (I see the tiger. I see the snake . . .). Then tell them that as they read new books, some will take on more complex patterns and then, increasingly, their books won't be patterned at all. Instead, the books will fall into a different category: stories.

Tell this group that when they read stories, in addition to using snap word power, they can use story knowledge to help them read. Teach them that stories usually begin by introducing who is in the story, where they are, and what they are doing. The characters may talk to each other, and there may be a little problem that gets solved at the end.

You can then set these kids up to revisit *The Carrot Seed*, a story they heard earlier in the year, to see whether these things play out—whether the author introduces the characters in the story, where they are, and what they are doing, early on. Then they could look through their book baggies, dividing their books into piles of stories and lists. The goal here is that they begin to notice when a book is a list and when it is a story so that they know which kind of power and knowledge to draw on when reading.

(continues)

MID-WORKSHOP TEACHING   Finding New Snap Words

I stood at the word wall and called out, "Readers, can I stop you for a minute?" When all eyes were on me, I said, "I am so impressed! You are not letting these harder books slow you down! You have snap word power to help you.

"Did you know that snap words are one of the biggest sources of power as you become older, more experienced readers? Here's why. The more you read, the more you see words. And the words you see over and over eventually become snap words. Reading and rereading pattern books has turned your brains into snap word machines!

"Right now, point to a word that you are seeing over and over again as you read that has become a snap word for you." I waited for the students to point to words and shared some of these with the class.

"Let's take a minute to read the word wall to *rev* up your snap word machines!" We did a shared reading of the word wall and then I said, "Power on! Keep reading."

TRANSITION TO PARTNER TIME
Partners Reread to Read More Smoothly

"Readers, it is partner time." I waited until I had their attention. "Just like when your training wheels come off your bike and you ride a bit wobbly at first, when you read harder books your reading might be a bit wobbly." I pretended that I was wobbling while riding a bike.

"When you are working hard to read lots of words on a page, it helps to go back and reread to smooth your reading out. As you restack your books for partner time, put the books that made your reading wobbly on the very top. You can reread those books first with your partner and smooth them out. Don't worry, you will be up and riding—er, I mean reading smoothly—soon!" I said, pretending to ride a bike smoothly.

You might wrap up this small group by telling the kids that when they get ready to read a book, it helps to think what kind of book it is, and if it's a story, to use what they know about how stories go to help them read those books.

Every day, your conferring will support individuals, small groups, and also partners. You might, for example, approach a particular day intent on checking in with partners. Even during private reading time, you could ask kids to read as partners so you can watch and support that important work.

When you observe partners reading together, you'll want to notice what they do with independence. Do they pile their books up on one side of their reading mat and proceed to read through the books, one after another? Do they put the easier books on the top of their pile? Do they talk about how they will read today and consider a few options, sometimes deciding to echo read, sometimes to see-saw read, and sometimes to play a reading game?

Notice, too, how effectively they work together.

◆ Do partners listen to one another?

◆ Do they divide reading time somewhat equally?

◆ Do they let each other have time to work at something before rushing in to help?

◆ Do partners have conversations that deepen an idea?

As in any conference, you will want to notice what partners are doing well and compliment that. If you see students who are organized but could use support coaching each other, you might say, "Readers! I noticed that you made a plan today for your reading by stacking up your books and having a book talk. That's what readers do."

Then, of course, you will also want to teach them something that pertains not only to this book and this day but to other books and other days. You might say something like "I want to remind you that when you are working together, it's your job to help coach your partner *through* the tricky parts. You can say things like 'Do the picture and the words match?' or 'Get your mouth ready to say this sound.'" You might add, "You can help each other by *not* telling your partner the tricky words. That's no fun when someone just gives you the answer while you are working hard to figure it out yourself!"

Turning Words into Snap Words

Introduce high-frequency words that appear often in higher-level texts.

I gathered the class in the meeting area. I stood at the word wall and said, "Readers, as you begin to read more challenging books, you are going to find more challenging snap words! You need to turn on those snap word machines in your brain!" I pretended to flick a switch. "One word that you will see *a lot* is the word *said*. Authors use this word to tell us when a character is talking. Let's use your snap word machines and transform *said* into a snap word! For this task, we will need to look closely while we read, spell, and write this snap word."

I jotted down the word *said* on an index card and placed it on the document camera. "Let's rev up those snap word machines. Zoooom in and look at it closely. What do you notice? Is it long? Short? Does it have tall letters? Short letters? Let's study it carefully. Turn and tell your partner what you notice about the word *said*.

"One fun way to turn a word into a snap word is to dribble and shoot the word like we are playing basketball!" I pretended to dribble a basketball as I spelled, "*S-a-i-d*," (one bounce for each letter) and then I pretended to shoot the ball as I said, "Said!" I had the class do this with me several times.

"Now write it in the air." The children wrote and spelled the word in the air.

"Let's look closely at it again. Try to take a picture of the word in your brain." I motioned with my hands as if I were holding a camera and taking a picture.

"Now, let's try to *read* it in our book, *Wake up, Dad*." I placed the book on the document camera, and we finished reading the book together, noticing the word *said* as we read.

After finishing the book, I added the new snap word to the word wall.

Readers Can Read Snap Words with Inflected Endings

IN THIS SESSION, you'll teach children that they can read familiar high-frequency words no matter what—even when they have inflected endings.

GETTING READY

✔ Select a leveled book that contains high-frequency words with common inflected endings, such as -s, -ing, and -ed, and contractions, or use the story *Hide and Seek*, by Lila. Another text we recommend is *Kitty Cat and Fat Cat* (Rigby) (see Teaching).

✔ Prepare an extra-strength icon to add to your "We Are Super Readers!" chart. The extra-strength icon is available on the online resources (see Link).

✔ Refer to your "Readers Read with a Partner" chart (see Transition to Partner Time).

✔ Prepare a set of magnetic letters to make the words *looked*, *going*, and *plays* (see Share).

MINILESSON

CONNECTION

Tell a story about not recognizing someone very familiar to you because the person wore something new. This will be a metaphor for ways that word endings can disguise familiar words.

"Readers, let me tell you a story." With wide eyes, and in my best storyteller's voice, I began my tale. "Yesterday, I walked up to my apartment, and there, standing outside my door, was a stranger! I didn't know who she was or what she was doing there. She had on a dark coat and a hat. I was nervous. What did this stranger want at my house?

"At first I didn't want to go near her, but then I thought, 'Hey, this is *my* house!' So I walked a little closer, and guess what?" I paused briefly to let the children's thoughts about the story run wild.

"It was my *mom*, in a *hat*. I clutched my forehead and shook my head to show just how silly I'd been, and the children laughed. "I didn't recognize *my mom*, a person I know *by heart*!

"I realized that the reason I didn't recognize this person who I know so well is that she'd put on a hat. She looked at little different. I'm not used to seeing her in a hat, so I didn't recognize her."

❖ **Name the teaching point.**

"And *this* is what I want to teach you, readers. There are words that you know by heart—your snap words. But you don't always recognize them because authors sometimes change them around a bit. When a word looks like a stranger to you—look again. You can ask yourself, does this look like another word that I know? It might be a familiar snap word wearing not a new hat, but a new ending."

TEACHING

Demonstrate recognizing a known word with an inflected ending and then reading the new word.

"I'll show you what I mean. But first, turn on your snap word machine." I flicked an imaginary switch, "and give it *extra strength*." I twisted the dial, and I watched as the children did the same.

"Okay, ready? If I get to a word that seems like a stranger has come into the story, watch as I ask myself, 'Does this look like a word that I *do* know?'"

I revealed the first page of the book under the document camera. "This is a true story called 'Hide and Seek,' by Lila, a first-grade writer across the hall. Let me read the first page on my own, okay? I'm going to pretend to be a kindergarten reader and use my extra-strength snap word power." I pointed under the words as I read the title and the first two words. I stopped at *playing*.

> I was
>
> playing
>
> hide and seek
>
> with Dad.

"Oh, hmm, . . . Gosh, this is a long word. Wait! Does this look like a word that I know? Don't tell me, I want to strengthen my own snap word power. It does! I see the word *play* at the beginning, and I know just *play* wouldn't sound right there. We are play—no. What would sound right? *Play-ing*! I slid my finger across the word to the end. Thumbs up if you thought *playing* too!" Thumbs and smiles popped up all around.

Name the strategy and demonstrate once again.

"Graduates, did you see how, when I got to a challenging word, I used my extra-strength snap word power to read a snap word with its ending? You did? Okay, keep watching, because I'll practice that work again."

> "Here he comes!"
>
> I said.

I kept reading and stopped again at *comes*. "Hmm, . . . does this look like a word I know? I waited a moment for children to think just to themselves, then answered my own question. "Yes, I recognize *come* at the beginning, and I can move my

Inflected endings can pose difficulty for readers, both visually and syntactically. It can be helpful to begin your focus using known words with inflected endings, because readers won't have to problem-solve the base word.

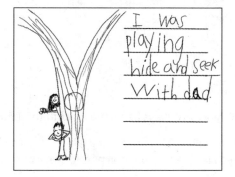

FIG. 15–1 *Hide and Seek* by Lila

eyes to the end—*comes*. Yes! 'Here he comes!' That makes sense in this story! And it sounds right too." I continued reading to the end of the page.

ACTIVE ENGAGEMENT

Give children the opportunity to read high-frequency words with inflected endings.

"You look ready to try this out, graduates! All right, here is the last page of the story. Read it with your partner and find out what happens to the girl in the game! And remember, if you get to a word that you don't know, use your extra-strength snap word power! Ask yourself, "Does it look like a word that I *do* know? Is it just a snap word with an ending on it?"

> Dad looked and looked.
>
> "I got you!" Dad said.

I listened in as partners read, and coached them to recognize the high-frequency words in continuous text and to make meaning of the story. "Eyes on me, graduates!" I called them back. "Well, your snap word power certainly did gain extra strength! I heard some of you say that *looked* was tough, but when you recognized *look*, you read the word to the end in a snap!"

LINK

Remind readers that they can always be on the lookout for familiar words when they face a reading challenge.

"Show me your extra-strength snap word power again, graduates." The children obliged, turning their imaginary dials. As they did this, I added an extra-strength icon next to snap word power on our chart.

"You are going to need that extra strength because your regular snap word power may not be enough to meet the challenges in your books. Remember, if you get to a word you do not know, you can always ask yourself, 'Do I know a word that looks like this word?' You might recognize a snap word there with an ending. Off you go, graduates!" And they moved to their reading spots, twisting the dials on their snap word machines.

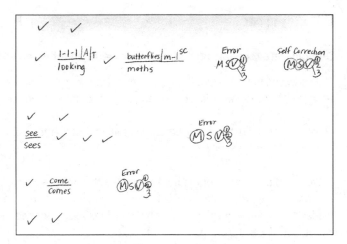

FIG. 15–2 This teacher took a quick running record as he listened to a child read her independent book. After doing a miscue analysis, the teacher realized that this reader would benefit from the work of this lesson.

To know words, readers need instruction on those words both in isolation (words only) and in context (in a book). In an earlier share, you worked on word endings in isolation, as you worked to break the base word from the -s ending. Often a reader can do this work in isolation but can still find it difficult to read the same word in continuous text, or vice versa. For this reason, you'll want to ensure that you work on words in both spheres. Today's share will once again allow for more practice in isolation.

Follow-Up Small Group on Hearing Sounds in Words

I N BEND II you probably worked with children who needed additional support with phonemic awareness. Be sure to check in with these readers and plan for follow-up sessions in which you add letter work. As you noticed, this work focused on hearing the sounds in words. According to research, effective phonemic awareness instruction happens when it is coupled with letter work (*Literacy Lessons Designed for Individuals*, Marie Clay, 2005). This helps children to use what their eyes can see to help make letter-sound connections, a fundamental step in learning to read. You will want to use the same Elkonin boxes and model how you place a letter(s) in each box for each sound you say and hear. So as you say cccccaaaaaattttt, write the letter *c* as you are saying /c/, the letter *a* when you get to /a/, and lastly, the letter *t* as you are saying /t/.

c	a	t

cccccccccccccaaaaaaaaaaaaaaaaaattttttttttttttttttttt

t	oy

ttttttttttttttttttttttttttttttttttooooooooooooyyyyyy

Let the student take over writing the letter that goes with the sound, and be ready to step in and write in the letter if the child does not know the visual representation. They are building their letter identification skills and knowledge of how they are connected to sounds from reading text and writing messages.

You will then want to transfer this work to the texts that students are reading. As you read with the child, you can look for objects to name in the pictures. Have the child say the word slowly, and record the letters that make the sounds. You will want to be careful not to interrupt too much of the reading, selecting only a couple words to work on, or choosing to do this activity after reading the text.

MID-WORKSHOP TEACHING
Recognizing Familiar Words and Familiar Endings

"Readers, I am going to pause your reading for just a moment. Thumbs up if you've been finding your snap words wearing a hat, er, I mean snap words with a new ending." Thumbs went up around the classroom. "Let's name some! Turn to a page where you recognized a snap word with an ending, and put a thumb up again when you are ready to share."

The children named *liked*, *running*, and *played*.

"Now, has anyone found these same endings on *other* words in your books? Oh! A few of you were rereading *My Bug Box*, one of our shared reading books, and found the word *stayed*. And some of you noticed *washed* when you were rereading *Itsy Bitsy Spider*!

"Not only can we get to know snap words by heart, but we can start to know some of these endings by heart too. That will help us when they are in other new words. Okay, graduates, dive back into your reading!"

TRANSITION TO PARTNER TIME
Extra-Strength Snap Word Hunt

"It's partner time!" I walked to the "Readers Read with a Partner" chart and touched "Hunt for snap words." "If you choose to do a snap word hunt with your partner today, you might not be hunting for snap words on their own. You might also be on the hunt for snap words with endings. We can call it an extra-strength snap word hunt! Go ahead, partners!"

Taking Words Apart with Common Endings

Work with known words to help children manipulate common word endings.

Once we were gathered back in the meeting area, I began, "Readers, to keep growing our snap word strength, we are going to practice taking apart some snap words with the endings you know."

Sitting next to the easel, I said, "Call out the letters as you see them go up on the easel. Then read the word when I slide my finger under it." One by one, I put up the letters in *look* on the magnetic board.

"*L! O! O! K!*" the children called out. "Now read the word," I said, as I ran my finger under the word. The children called out, "Look!" and I nodded.

"You know that sometimes snap words look diferent. Some of you found this ending in your books earlier today. What is this ending? Say the letters." I put up an *e* and a *d* at the end of *look* and the children named the two letters.

"Sometimes the *ed* ending can sound like /t/, and the word sounds like this: *look*," and I slid the word to the left, "/t/." I slid the *ed* together over to the end of *look*. Running my finger under the word, I read *looked* out loud and then asked the children to read it.

We followed these same steps to make *going* (first making *go* and then adding *-ing*) and *plays* (first putting up *play* and then adding *-s*), before I reminded the children, "Remember, readers, be sure to read your snap words all the way to the end. They may have endings hiding there!"

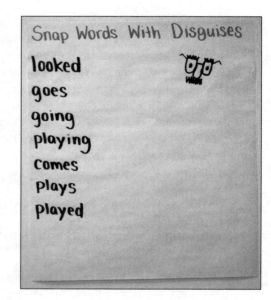

FIG. 15–3   A collection of snap words with endings found by readers

Readers Use All They Know about Stories to Make Predictions

MINILESSON

CONNECTION

IN THIS SESSION, you'll teach children that knowing how stories go can help them read and think about what might happen next.

Highlight that the children's books are changing. Not all of their books are lists and patterns. Now more of their books are stories.

"Readers, thumbs up if you remember that poem that we've been reading, *Oh, the Places You'll Go!*"

I placed *Wake up, Dad* under the document camera as I said, "Well, I've been thinking about the places *you* will go now that you are reading stories like this one." I began pointing under the words, signaling for kids to join in, as we read aloud the first few familiar pages.

"Now that you bring so many powers to your reading, you are reading lots of different kinds of books, and just like you, the books you are reading keep growing and changing. You read lots of books that are lists or patterns that sound like this: The boy likes to run. The boy likes to jump. The boy likes to climb."

Tell children that the stories they find in their books are just like the ones they wrote in writing workshop.

Now that you are graduating to new books, remember that *some* books are still lists and patterns, but sometimes, you'll open a book and find in it," and I began tapping my hands on the sides of the chair to create a drumroll, "a story—just like the true stories you wrote in writing workshop!"

❖ Name the teaching point.

"Today I want to teach you that when you read a book that is a story, it will tell about a person (or an animal), and that person will do one thing and then the next thing," I said, listing across my fingers as I talked, "and finally, the story will end."

GETTING READY

✔ Plan to reference and use *Wake up, Dad*, by Beverley Randell, or a similar familiar text (see Connection and Share).

✔ Select a text at, or slightly above, the current benchmark level. You will want to choose a book similar to *Wake up, Dad*. You can use a big book or place the book under the document camera (see Teaching and Active Engagement).

✔ Select a familiar text that is a story to work on retelling. We return to *Wake up, Dad* (see Share).

✔ Prepare a new chart titled "Super Readers Retell!" You will use this chart to teach readers the important things to include when they retell a story (see Share). 👏

TEACHING AND ACTIVE ENGAGEMENT

Engage children in thinking about how the start of the story can help them think about the next part.

"Readers, when you read a story, it's not just the pictures and words on the page that help you read. Your thinking about the story helps you too. If I wrote a story that started like this: The little girl dropped her ice cream cone on the ground. What do you think might happen next?"

Some kids called out, "She started to cry." Others said, "She picked it up."

I nodded. "You see? Your thinking is helping you even before you look at the picture or the words."

"Let's try it again. What if I wrote another story that went like this: It was my birthday. I walked in the room. I saw a lot of kids and a big cake. The kids jumped up and . . . What do you think might come next?"

"They all started singing Happy Birthday!" the children chanted in unison.

"You see? When you read a story, you don't just wait for the words and the picture to tell you what comes next! Your brain tells you too. The start of the story helps you to think about and maybe know the next part of it."

Channel the children to try the strategy with you in a leveled text from the classroom library.

"Let's try this in a book together." I placed a leveled text from the classroom library under the document camera and said, "This is a book just like so many of the books in your book baggies." I pointed to the title as I read it aloud and briefly talked about the front cover. I turned the page and the children chimed in and read along.

After reading the first few pages, I paused and said, "Let's stop for a minute and think about what's happened so far in this story. Give me a thumbs up when you have some ideas about what might happen in the next part." After a moment, I prompted the children to turn and talk, making sure to recap some of the things I heard the children share with their partners.

We read the next few pages together before stopping again. I prompted the children to think about the next part, "What do you think might happen next?" The children turned to share their ideas. I listened in and voiced back what I had heard. Then, we read the next page to confirm or revise.

Notice the connection to writing workshop. You are using this as an entry point to support reading. During the Writing for Readers unit of study, the children learned about personal narrative writing. It is important to help children transfer this knowledge to the books they are reading. When writing personal narratives, your children learned that a story is not a list. Rather, something happens and it moves through time in sequence.

In this minilesson you will notice that the children start doing the work with you at the beginning of the teaching. The method used for the teaching and active engagement in this minilesson is guided practice. With this method you are thinking alongside the students, coaching with quick lean prompts, giving children multiple opportunities to practice the strategy.

LINK

Recap the teaching of today's minilesson, reminding children to use all they know about how stories go to help as they are reading.

"Readers, using everything you know about stories can help you think about and understand your books even more. Remember, don't just wait for the pictures and words to tell you what happens. Use your brain and everything you are thinking about the story to help you too.

"When you are reading stories, don't forget to stop and think, 'What might happen next?' Then keep reading to find out. Off you go, graduates!"

During reading time today, you may notice that some children approximate the work of this minilesson, and it will be difficult for you to observe other children doing this. Either way, it is still important for you to highlight that you observed children trying this work. When you do this, it becomes a suggestion that helps children feel successful and encourages them to role-play themselves into the readers they will soon become.

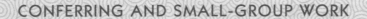

Supporting Readers Who Are Ready to Move Up Reading Levels

AS YOU ARE NEARING THE END OF THE UNIT you may find that some of your readers are ready to work with more challenging texts. These may be your students who are flying through their books, without pausing. They may be the first to shout out words in your shared reading texts or are increasingly off-task during private reading time. Perhaps you find that in your conferring, these students are making few, if any, decoding errors and can retell their books with increasing accuracy. You might use your conferring time to assess students' reading levels. When children appear ready to move up levels you can conduct some running records on books from their book baggies or a book you bring with you to the conference. You may want to have a short stack of leveled texts from your library to use for these quick assessments. Ask a child to read aloud, and mark her miscues and self-corrections.

One thing you will want to determine is which cueing systems the student uses most often, and which she may not be calling on. If you hear a child read, "The dog jumps on the sofa," instead of "The dog jumps on the couch," that child is using meaning cues and ignoring visual information. You will want to teach this child to notice the beginning and ending sounds of words, making sure that what she says matches what she sees on the page. If, instead, you notice that the reader is sacrificing meaning but attending to the letters in unknown words, for example, reading "The dog jumps on the catch" instead of *couch*, you will want to work with that reader on monitoring for meaning, making sure that the words she says make sense in the sentence and with what is happening in the story. A third cueing system you will want to check for is syntax. If you hear readers reading words that do correlate with English sentence structure, perhaps leaving off inflected endings or reading words in the wrong tense, you may prompt by asking, "Does that sound right?"

MID-WORKSHOP TEACHING
Remembering to Make Predictions Along the Way

"Readers, give me your eyes." The children gave me their attention. "I was watching as you were reading today, and I saw some of you stop for *just* a moment. It was so fast, I almost missed it. You put your books down and sort of looked up, like this." I mimed glancing up contemplatively, rubbing my chin to exaggerate a *thinking* pose.

"It was almost like I could see a thinking bubble grow over your heads! I'm guessing that as you were reading, you were pausing, ever so quickly, to think, 'Hmm, . . . what might happen next?' And you didn't just do it *one* time in your book. You stopped to think like that a few times in each book! Tap your mind if you were doing that work." Children all around began tapping their heads.

"Remember, you can do that all the time when you read! You can think, 'What might happen next?' not just one time, but lots of times across your books. All right, readers, get right back to reading—and thinking!"

TRANSITION TO PARTNER TIME
Asking Partners to Make Predictions

"Readers, it is partner time!" I called from the middle of the classroom. "Since you've been working hard to use your brain *and* the pictures with the words to learn what happens next in your books, you might want to play 'Guess What's Next!' with your partner today! Maybe this time, if you choose a book from your baggie that your partner hasn't read yet, *you* can ask your partner that question! As you are reading the book, you can ask, 'What do you think might happen next?' and then your partner can share her thinking. Enjoy your partner reading!"

In addition to assessing a child's miscues, you will want to assess fluency and comprehension. Jot down a few notes about fluency as soon as the child is finished reading. Then ask the child to retell the book and answer a few comprehension questions. Use this information to determine strengths and next steps for the child.

You might also pull a small group of readers who are reading level C–E texts and are ready to strengthen their retells by discussing the characters' feelings. You can use *Wake up, Dad* or the familiar text that you used in the minilesson to model this for the small group and then have them try it with a book from their book baggie. Or make plans to support a group of readers reading level F/G books. You may notice that these readers need support maintaining meaning in these longer texts. As you listen in to their reading, prompt them to accumulate the text by saying, "Tell what has happened so far."

Readers Retell Stories

Teach students to retell stories by looking back to the cover, saying the title, and saying what happened across the pages (including who, where, and what).

I sang the class gathering song as the children put away their book baggies and made their way to the meeting area. Once the children had gathered, I began. "Readers, you can use what you know about stories to help you understand your books even more. And do you know what? You can do this while you are reading, and you can even do it when you are finished reading. Sometimes when you finish a book, you can retell it to yourself or your partner.

"Thumbs up if you remember how to retell books." Thumbs popped up in the air. "When we retell books, we say the title, what it is about, and talk about the ending. Right? Well, since you have graduated, and so many of your powers needed to change, your retells need to change too—especially if you are retelling a story.

"When you retell stories, you look back to the cover, say the title, and say what happened across the pages." I gestured to the new chart and said, "And just like you tell *who*, *where*, and *what* when you write a story, you also include those important things when you retell a story."

I placed *Wake up, Dad* under the document camera and quickly flipped through the pages before prompting the class to retell the book. I coached partnerships with this work, nudging children to add in characters' feelings. After everyone had an opportunity to practice, I voiced back some of the things I heard, highlighting some of the children who had included characters' feelings.

I made notes in my plans for the children to continue practicing this skill in shared reading, read-aloud, and reading workshop. I also made a note to add "tell feelings" to the chart in the next few days, knowing that I'd explicitly teach this to the class in the upcoming week.

"So whenever you finish reading a book, remember that you can retell the book to yourself or your partner before you read a new book. And if you are retelling a story, remember to talk about *who*, *where*, and *what*."

FIG. 16–1   Chart to support retelling

Readers Need Extra-Strength Reread Power to Bring Their Books to Life

MINILESSON

In your connection, you might remind your students of the work they did in the previous unit to help bring their books to life. You might say, "Readers, do you remember how great you were at making your books come to life? You all learned how to read your books with your smoothest reading voice, just like a grown-up would read to you!" Then hold up a simple patterned text and say, "That was pretty easy to do in a book like this!" You might model reading a few simple pages with lots of expression. Then open a book with significantly more text on the page. You could say, "But now that you are reading more challenging books, sometimes you are working *so hard* turning up all your powers to read that you forget to use your reading voice to bring your books to life." You'll want to remind your students that they can always try to make their reading sound great, especially when they reread a familiar book. Lean in close and offer to give them a tip.

Then, name the teaching point. Say, "Today I want to teach you that to *really* make your books come to life you can reread them, *thinking* about what's happening. On each page, you can think about what's going on and then read it in a voice that matches."

During your teaching, you'll want to demonstrate how readers do this with a familiar text. For example, you might return to *Wake up, Dad* and, turning to page 6, pause to model the thinking you are doing. You might say, "All the kids got up, and now Kate wants to try to wake up Dad. She *really* wants Dad to get up, but it looks like Dad just wants to sleep. Let me try reading it so that my voice matches that idea and sounds just like Kate talking and Dad talking." You could then read in a choppy monotone voice and prompt kids to give you feedback. "Did that sound like Kate *really* wanted Dad to get up? No? Let me reread it!" This time read the page expressively, changing your voice to match each character in the book. You might even recruit your readers to try it with you a third time.

For your active engagement, turn to another page in the book and give the students a chance to try this work. For example, you might turn to page 14. Prompt partners first to turn and talk to share their thinking about the page. You'll want to coach your readers to say who's in the picture, what they are doing, and also how they might be feeling in that part. Highlight some comments to share with the group such as "Kate tried to wake up Dad, James tried to wake up Dad, Nick tried to wake up Dad, and now Mom is coming too. They are all going to try to wake him up together! I bet they're getting frustrated!" Then encourage the class to read the page together, making their voices match. You'll want to reread the page several times, perhaps noting the bold print and using it as a clue for how the last line might sound different.

In your link, remind your readers that even now that they have graduated to more challenging books that need a lot of extra-strong reading powers, they still have to remember that it's their responsibility to make their reading sound the best it can. This helps bring their books to life. Encourage them to do this especially *every* time they reread a favorite book!

CONFERRING AND SMALL-GROUP WORK

As you confer and pull small groups, you'll want to remember to divide your time between small-group work and conferences. You may choose to do a couple of guided reading groups, perhaps following up with students who have recently moved into new levels of text. You'll also want to spend some time coaching readers in reading with more fluency. You'll want to be aware of students reading around level D who are consistently looking closely at words and letters but still using their finger to point as they read. These children are ready to remove their finger from the text, and as soon as they do so, you'll notice a dramatic improvement in their fluency. Encourage these children to read with their eyes using their finger at points of difficulty and make their reading sound like talking. On the other hand, you'll want to be mindful of any readers having difficulty attending to visual information. These children may still need to point to the text for a little while longer.

Mid-Workshop Teaching

During your mid-workshop teaching, show your readers how *thinking* about their books and reading in a voice that matches is a way to turn up their reread power. Teach children that each time they reread, they know their book a little better, and this helps them to think a little more about what's happening. Then it's even easier to make your voice match. You might decide to add an extra-strength icon to the "We have reread power" Post-it on your chart. Then have students take out the book they just finished reading and reread it, thinking even more about what's happening on each page and working hard to make their voices match.

Transition to Partner Time

When you transition to partner time, suggest that partners can help each other to do this work, perhaps by reading aloud to each other. Partners could talk about a page together and then take turns reading the page with their most expressive voices. While one partner reads, the other partner could listen and then give a little tip if needed. After rereading the page, partners could change roles on the next page, one person being the reader and the other the listener.

SHARE

During today's share, you might teach children that authors use punctuation marks to give the reader little tips for how to read their books. Remind them of the learning they did in the previous unit, watching out for ending punctuation. Then tell students that there is another punctuation mark that is very helpful to readers, especially in more challenging books: quotation marks! Point these out in your demonstration text and teach your readers that these are a clue that somebody is about to talk. You might say, "Readers, you've got to watch carefully, and as soon as you see quotation marks, get ready to change your voice and make it sound like talking!" Try this out together on a couple pages in your demonstration text, using the picture to think about who might be talking and how they would talk. Then end your reading workshop by returning to your demonstration text to do a shared reading of the book from beginning to end. As you read, pause occasionally to point out quotation marks and to remind your readers to think about what's happening and make their voice match. If you have time, you might even read the book a second time, this time assigning groups of students to be each character in the book, turning your shared reading into a little readers' theater. "Wow!" you might say as you finish the book. "Your reading made me feel like I was *right* there in the room laughing when Dad finally fell out of bed. You turned up your reread power to make your reading sound great, and it brought the book to life!"

Readers Need Extra-Strength Book Talk Power

IN THIS SESSION, you'll teach children new ways they can think and talk about their books. Because their books and powers have grown and changed, so too does the way they should talk about books.

GETTING READY

✔ Cue the song "Pomp and Circumstance" on a music player (see Connection).

✔ Display your "We Are Super Readers!" chart (see Connection).

✔ Display the book *Oh, the Places You'll Go!* to reference during the minilesson (see Connection).

✔ Choose a familiar text that is at or above the current benchmark. You will use this book to demonstrate ways readers can strengthen their book talk power. The book you select should allow you to talk more about the characters and their feelings. We use *Wake up, Dad*, by Beverley Randell, but this text is easily interchangeable with others (see Teaching).

✔ Have children bring a familiar storybook from their book baggie to the meeting area for today's minilesson (see Active Engagement).

✔ Prepare an extra-strength icon for your "We Are Super Readers!" chart. The extra-strength icon is available on the online resources (see Link).

✔ Make sure Post-its are in children's book baggies (see Mid-Workshop Teaching).

✔ Have your "Super Readers Retell!" chart available to refer to. You will add "Tell feelings" to the chart (see Mid-Workshop Teaching).

✔ Display your "Readers Read with a Partner" chart (see Transition to Partner Time).

✔ Prepare "Oh, the Books We Will Read!," a poem about growing readers based on *Oh, the Places You'll Go!* (see Share).

✔ Display the "Hooray!" poem (see Share).

MINILESSON

CONNECTION

Celebrate the fact that so many reading powers have graduated and now have extra strength.

As the graduation song began to play, the children proudly paraded around the room and made their way to the meeting area.

Once I had the attention of the class, I gestured to the "We Are Super Readers!" chart and leaned forward, saying, "Last night I realized that not only have *you* become stronger and more grown up since the beginning of the year (and this unit), but so have *all* of your reading powers. Just look at our super powers chart. You have turned up your picture power, snap word power, your reread power, and *even* sound power!" I gestured turning up a dial as the children did the same. "All of this new strength is helping you read so many new books."

Tell children that since the books they are reading have changed, their book talk power also needs to grow and change. It is ready to graduate.

"So here's the important thing for you to know; since your powers and books keep growing and changing, the way you *think* and *talk* about your books also needs to grow and change." I pointed to the partner chart as I said, "You have actually become experts at talking about some parts of your books, like favorite parts or funny parts, and even surprising parts. But *now*, I think you are ready to do even *more*! *Now* you are ready to bring extra strength to your book talk power. You are ready to graduate to new things and more ways to think and talk about your books."

I gestured to *Oh, the Places You'll Go!* on the easel beside me, and chanted the first stanza out loud.

The children chimed in as they puffed out their chests and flexed their muscles.

❧ Name the teaching point.

"Today I want to teach you that after you use all of your extra-strength powers to read your books, you can think and talk even more about them. When you finish a book, sometimes you and your partner can talk more about the book and the characters. You might even talk about what the characters are doing or how they feel and why they feel that way."

TEACHING

Use a familiar text to demonstrate a nonexample and then pause to remember that your book talk power has graduated. It has extra strength; you can talk more about a book and the characters.

"Right now I am going to need your help. I am going to need all of you to pretend you are my partner and that we just finished reading this storybook together. Pretend that we are sitting hip to hip."

I placed *Wake up, Dad* on the document camera as I quickly flipped through some of the pages. After I read the last page aloud, I closed the book abruptly, placed my hands on my hips and quickly said, "I liked it. Did you? Okay, ready to read another book?"

A few children blurted out, "No Way! We need to talk about it!"

"You're right! Thanks for reminding me that we need to use our extra-strength powers to talk more about the characters, what they are doing, what they are feeling, and why they feel that way."

Demonstrate going back to an important part in the book to think about the characters and story events, making sure to find information in the pictures and words to support your idea(s).

I turned to the last page of the book and tapped the picture as I said, "Let's talk about the ending. Do you have some ideas? Just look at Kate, Nick, James, and even Mom. I think they are really excited, and even a little surprised, that they got Dad out of bed. They tried so hard to wake Dad up, and at the end they finally got him out of bed. And just look at James. He has a huge grin on his face and he is pumping his fists in the air—like he is cheering and really proud of their accomplishment."

I giggled aloud as I said, "Well, I wonder how Dad feels about getting woken up and pulled out of bed. Talk to your partner about your ideas.

"My goodness! Our book talk power just got so strong. Now it has extra strength. Before we read another book, we talked more about the book and the characters. Because *all* of our powers have extra strength, we knew that we could also talk more about the characters."

Children reading level B–E books with characters should be prompted to use the pictures and words to talk not only about who is in the story and what they are doing, but also how they feel and why they feel that way. Children reading level F–H books will need to do more envisioning in addition to using the pictures and words. Remember that children have been doing this work during read-aloud and shared reading since the beginning of the year.

There are many things you can do to make your demonstrations more effective. To help with pacing, you should limit the amount of text used to demonstrate, remembering that you don't need to read the whole book. This is one of the reasons to use a demonstration text that is familiar to your students, especially in minilessons similar to this one.

ACTIVE ENGAGEMENT

Coach the children as they talk more about a familiar storybook from their book baggie.

"You're ready to try this new extra-strength power. Go ahead and get out the book you brought with you. Before we talk with our partners, take a minute to reread some of the important parts you want to talk about. Study the pictures to think more about the book and characters. You might even think about what the characters are doing, how they feel, and why they feel that way.

"When you are ready, Partner 2, you can start."

Use generalizable prompts to coach partnerships as they talk more about their books and find information to support their ideas.

I stood up and began moving around the meeting area, coaching partnerships with prompts such as "What are you thinking?" "Say more about that," "Why do you think that?" "Do you have any other ideas?" and "Show your partner the part of the book that makes you think that."

After both partners had the opportunity to share their thinking, I sat back down and said, "Wow! Not only does your book talk power have extra strength, but so does your partner power. I didn't just hear you talking more about your books. I also saw you listening carefully and heard you saying, 'I think . . . ,' 'Maybe . . . ,' and 'I wonder . . .' after your partner talked about their book."

LINK

Remind readers that there are different reasons to reread. Readers might reread to smooth out their reading or to mark places they want to talk about more with their partner.

"Today when you are reading, you might decide to reread a book after you finish it. You can reread to make your reading sound smooth, and you can also reread to mark places where you want to use your extra-strength book talk power to talk about your book during partner time." I added the extra-strength icon to "book talk power" on the chart.

"If you have a storybook, you can think more about the characters, what they are doing, their feelings, and why they feel that way. Remember that studying the pictures can help you think and talk more about your books. Off you go, book talk graduates!"

EXTRA STRENGTH!

If some children are holding information books, you might channel them to choose books from their baggies that have characters.

Remember that readers will have a variety of texts in their book baggies during this unit. It is likely that most readers will have a handful of books with familiar characters. Because readers will also have list books and nonfiction books, you will want to think about ways to support their talk and comprehension in these texts as well.

The work in this minilesson will be continued in shared reading, read-aloud, and throughout the remainder of the year.

Conferring with Partners

AS YOU MOVE AROUND THE ROOM to confer with readers, in addition to the small groups you see, you may want to help readers prepare for partner talk. You might, for example, ask readers what parts they plan to share with their partner and prompt them to mark those pages. You can then take the role of a "proficient partner" and engage in a book talk discussing what you think the characters are doing, how they feel, and why they feel that way. If readers have information books, you might teach them how to raise the level of talk in this kind of book. You could talk about what the book is teaching and have them mark pages with interesting information they are learning (from the words or the pictures) or questions they have to share with their partner.

You will want to confer with some readers during partner reading time. First, watch to see how a set of partners tends to work, and then coach into that in ways that establish better habits.

You could remind a particular partnership to use partner time (for now) as a time to tackle books that are one notch harder than those they have been reading during private time, which would mean the children read an entirely different set of books when they work together. You can then observe the readers as they problem solve together, and coach them in ways that are responsive. You might notice that these readers need reminders to get ready to read before diving into new books. Teach them to use the title, cover, and first few pages to think about how the book might go. During the first (or second) reading of these books, these partnerships might be working on word solving. If these readers are reading level C or D books and you notice they need support searching for meaning and visual information, you might prompt them by saying, "Look at the picture and get your mouth ready for the first letter(s)." You might also coach the partnership to think about what is happening and move their fingers across the word, going from the beginning to the end of the word.

(continues)

MID-WORKSHOP TEACHING
Remind Students to Prepare for Partner Time

"Readers, pause your reading for just a moment." The children put their books down and looked at me.

"It will be partner time soon, and I want to remind you to get ready to turn up your book talk power to extra strength! Choose a book that you want to talk more about. Reread some of the important parts that you want to tell your partner about, and mark those places with the Post-its in your baggies.

"Remember, if you are reading a story, you can get ready to talk about what the characters are doing, how they are feeling, and why they might feel that way!" As I talked, I pointed to our chart and added "Tell feelings."

Super Readers Retell!

- Tell who
- Tell where
- Tell what happened
- Tell it in order
- **Tell feelings**

I gave the children just a moment to begin to reread and mark a few parts in one of their books. "As you keep reading, you might decide to reread and mark parts to talk about in other books too! Okay, continue private reading!"

Readers Use All of Their Extra-Strength Book Talk Power

"It's partner time! Today, and from now on, after you decide *how* to read one of your books together, you might start by talking about your books! You can use the parts you marked with your Post-its to remind you about what you wanted to talk about, and you can even show those pages to your partner as you talk! All right, ready to turn up your partner power and book talk power to *extra strength?*" I twisted an imaginary dial, and the children did too, as they gathered their books to meet with their partners.

You could also support partners in talking about their books. In the previous units children were taught to talk about "wow" pages and funny and favorite parts of books. If you notice partners reading one book, then another, and then another without talking about their books, you can use this as a time to remind them that readers don't just *read* books together. They also *talk about* their books. After readers finish one book, they can think about a part they want to talk about and go to that part. Partners might even have more than one part they want to talk about before they start reading another book. You can also support comprehension by reminding these readers that they can use the last page or part to talk about what the book was about before reading another book together. Another option is to remind these readers that they can make their books come to life by acting them out.

As you confer with partnerships, you will want partners to face each other while you sit behind them to coach their talk. When one partner says their idea, you can whisper to the other partner, saying, "Say more about that," "Why do you think that?" "Do you have any other ideas?" and "Show me the part of the book that makes you think that." Then you can help them to keep the conversation going with prompts like "I think . . . ," "Maybe . . . ," and "I wonder . . ."

Choral Reading to Prepare for Celebration

Introduce the poem that will be read during tomorrow's celebration

When children had gathered on the rug, I said, "Readers, when I look at you, I no longer see the little kids you were at the start of this unit. I see bigger, stronger readers! You've worked so hard to turn up your reading powers!

"Tomorrow will be our graduation celebration. I wrote a poem for us to read to honor the day!"

I read the poem to the class and then asked them to choral read it.

> Hooray!
> Today is our day.
>
> We're off to great places.
> We're off and away!
>
> We have all that we need.
> We've turned up our powers!
>
> Oh, the books we will read.
> OH, THE BOOKS WE WILL READ!

Prepare children to choral read the poem for the final celebration and invite partners to team up and choral read the poem.

After we finished I leaned in and said, "You have become such strong readers, I don't think you will need me to lead you in reading this poem tomorrow. You can read chorally *with* your partner. But here's the thing: choral reading together can be tricky. Are you up for the challenge?" The class cheered. "I knew you would be! When you read with your partner, you have to read with your eyes *and* your ears. You have to listen to your partner and keep your voices together, just like we do in shared reading."

"Partners, you just turned up your partner power! Let's add choral reading to our partner reading chart!" I added the "Choral read" sticky note and the extra-strength icon to the partner chart.

FIG. 18–1   Shared reading to prepare for celebration

Readers Read with a Partner

Decide how to read.
- ECHO, Echo, echo read.
- See-saw read.
- **Choral read.**

Decide what to do.
- Add a pinch of you. (I think . . .)
- Give reminders to use POWERS!
- Hunt for snap words.
- Play "Guess What's Next!"
- Play "Alphabet Pop It!"

Choral read.

I handed each partnership a copy of the poem and coached them as they read, together. I reminded them to put it in their baggies and be ready to bring it back for our celebration.

Celebration

Readers Use All of Their Powers to Read New Books

MINILESSON

In your connection, you might start your minilesson by congratulating the class on all of the hard work they have done turning up their powers in this unit. You can lead the class in a shared reading of the super powers chart. You might want to return to *Oh, the Places You'll Go!* and read the first few lines.

Then, name the teaching point. Say, "Today I want to remind you that readers can't just use one or two powers when they read. They have to use *all* of their powers!"

In your teaching and active engagement, you might do a shared reading of *The Bug Box*. You might say something like "Readers, when we started this unit, we had so much fun reading this book together. You have become so much stronger as readers, I think you are ready to read it *without* me!" Let the kids chime in during the reading, only inserting your voice if the children need this support. You will want to have your anchor charts for the unit close by so you can stop and point to each power as you remind and encourage kids to use each strategy.

In your link, you will want to cheer kids on, reminding them that they have so many powers to read harder books. Then, send them off to read today, adapting a line from *Oh, the Places You'll Go!* You might say, "Readers, today is your day! Your books are waiting. So, get on your way!"

CONFERRING AND SMALL-GROUP WORK

As you circulate around the room to confer and work with small groups today, you will want to refer to the anchor charts, asking students to show you where they have tried some of the strategies in their reading. Make sure to celebrate all of their hard work. You'll also want to take note of the progress children have made. It is important that you have a clear understanding of what the next steps are for your readers and are ready to carry these forward. This will help you to move into the next unit with a plan of action ready for conferences and small groups that will help your students continue to grow.

Mid-Workshop Teaching

During your mid-workshop teaching, you will want to remind your readers about reread power and encourage them to reread the poem that they practiced yesterday so that they are ready for the celebration.

Transition to Partner Time

When you transition to partner time, students can work together to choral read the poem to get ready for the celebration. You will want to make sure to celebrate all of their partner power and encourage them to use their best reading voices.

SHARE

During today's share, you'll celebrate by having everyone bring the poem they have been practicing for the celebration. You might play "Pomp and Circumstance" as the class has a procession to the meeting area. If you have parents join you for the graduation, you could formally introduce the graduating class and give a little speech celebrating all of the hard reading work they have been doing. Have the class stand and read the poem together.

   After reading the poem, you might bring your celebration to a close with a reading of *Oh, the Places You'll Go!* or *I Can Read with My Eyes Shut*, by Dr. Seuss. You might even decide to give each child a diploma of some sort. You could roll up a printed copy of your favorite reading quote and tie it with a ribbon. You might use the Dr. Seuss quote, "The more that you read, the more things you will know. The more that you learn, the more places you'll go." Then you might formally call every child up, give him or her a scroll, and cheer for each one. If you went all out and made graduation caps for the class, they could throw their caps in the air!

   Hooray!

Read-Aloud

Getting Ready: BOOK SELECTION

For your interactive read-alouds across this unit and throughout the year, you will want to choose a combination of literature and informational texts. Interactive read-aloud is a time when children are exposed to rich literature and texts across genres. During this time, the teacher supports comprehension by modeling thinking work as she reads aloud expressively and fluently. You will want to select a text that will also support children as they develop their speaking and listening skills through partnership and whole-class conversations. While your shared reading is a time where the students are supported to read texts a few levels above what they can read independently, interactive read-aloud is a time when children can be exposed to more complex texts because they aren't asked to do any word-solving or fluency work (e.g., they don't have to attend to the print).

Similar to the picture books you were using in the previous two units, you will want to choose picture books that spotlight engaging characters and contain rich story language. We also recommend selecting informational texts that contain engaging photographs and illustrations that will help readers deepen their understanding of the text. Many teachers choose informational texts with content that aligns to their science and social studies curriculum or is a topic that is reflective of the interests of the

Dragonflies, by Margaret Hall

readers in their classroom. Choose picture books that are similar to *Knuffle Bunny*, by Mo Willems, *Whistle for Willie* and *The Snowy Day*, by Ezra Jack Keats, or *Koala Lou*, by Mem Fox. Choose informational texts that are similar to *Fishy Tales*, by DK Readers, *Diving Dolphin*, by Karen Wallace, or *National Geographic Readers: Trucks!*, by Wil Mara.

We chose *Dragonflies*, by Margaret Hall, because so many kindergarten children are fascinated by insects, bugs, animals, and the world around them. The photographs in the book are large, vibrant, and engaging. *Dragonflies* is one of the titles in the set *Bugs, Bugs, Bugs!* from Capstone Press. If you decide to read aloud other books from this set, readers will be able to work on similar skills and build their content knowledge around this topic. Capstone Press has several sets of texts around a variety of subjects and topics. If you are teaching an informational writing unit later in the year, this text can be used again as a mentor text for studying author's craft throughout that writing unit.

READ-ALOUD SESSIONS 1 AND 2

GOALS/Rationale/Prelude

◆ Similar to the interactive read-alouds during the last unit, you'll engage your students in various ways during this read-aloud, reading with an animated voice, thinking aloud, asking all the students to engage in conversations around the text, and prompting children to use reading skills. Remember to prompt children to look closely at the pictures, react and respond, chime in, and act out important parts throughout the read-aloud. Although you will read today's book from start to finish on Day One, we imagine you will return to this book for a variety of reasons and purposes across the unit (and in other units throughout the year).

◆ Across this unit, you will also be supporting readers as they continue to move into conventional reading. Your reading workshop minilessons will give readers explicit instruction around using the pattern of the text, reading known words in text automatically, and using some of the letters in a word along with meaning and syntax to problem solve and comprehend text. Readers will also be using the cover, title, and last part to retell and talk about their books. In addition to a variety of word study concepts, your daily shared reading time will be used to support and reinforce these comprehension, fluency, and word-solving skills.

◆ It is important to remember that your read-aloud time during this unit will be used to further support and develop comprehension skills and partner talk. You'll show kids the "whole" of how reading goes, planning times to stop and model the habits of proficient readers. You'll also plan for times when the children will both turn and talk and act out what they are reading. At the end of the reading, you will want to plan on engaging the children in a conversation around the text. Perhaps you will have the children use the photographs to retell what they learned in the book (many of the teachers we work with refer to this as "turning and teaching"). The children may also share some of their ideas or questions about the topic or check the predictions they made before reading. Whatever you plan for, it is important to remember one of the big purposes of the read-aloud time: to create a love of reading in addition to developing and supporting comprehension skills. This is a cherished and favorite time of day for all kindergarten teachers and students. Enjoy!

BEFORE YOU READ

Make sure the "Readers TALK about Books" chart is displayed in a place where the children will be able to easily reference it throughout the read-aloud.

Readers TALK about Books

"I notice . . ."
"I think . . ."
"I wonder . . ."
"What do you think?"

Throughout the read-aloud, you will want to listen in to assess students' thinking as well as their speaking and listening skills.

As you listen to the children, you will want to notice the skills they seem strong with and ones that need additional support. Notice how children are working and talking about the book together:

◆ Are students taking turns?

◆ Are students listening to each other?

◆ Are students using the picture/words read aloud to say what they notice?

◆ Are students sharing ideas? Asking questions?

Introduce the book by giving students the gist of the topic, discussing the table of contents, taking a picture walk of the first few pages, and setting a purpose for reading.

"This is a book called *Dragonflies*. It is a nonfiction book written by Margaret Hall, and the illustrations are really cool photographs. Let's look closely at the title and picture on the front cover. What do you think this book might teach us? Give me a thumbs up when you have some ideas.

"Let me check to see if there's more information on the back cover." Take a moment to turn to the back cover and quickly read aloud the information about dragonflies that is provided. Read aloud expressively and in an animated way. As you are reading, act out and put gestures to the information you are reading about.

"We know this book is about dragonflies and that dragonflies are a kind of insect, just like butterflies and bees. Let's take a look at the table of contents and study a few pictures to think about what Margaret Hall might teach us about dragonflies in this book." Quickly pause and think about the table of contents. Then scan over a few pages, perhaps through page 9 or 11, recruiting the kids to look closely and say aloud what they see in the photographs.

One possibility for shortening the read-aloud on this day is to begin reading right after you discuss the table of contents, rather than scanning a few pages and pictures.

In the table of contents, read aloud the names of the first three chapters and pause to think about what readers might learn about in this book.

Narrate the process of previewing by thinking about the chapters in the book and the information the author will teach in each section. "Hmm, . . . One part of this book is about what dragonflies look like, and another part is about what dragonflies do. Are you getting some more ideas about what Margaret Hall might want to teach us in this book? I know I am. I just can't wait to read it."

Pages 4–11: Recruit children to look closely at the photographs and discuss what they notice.

Stop on pages 4 and 5. "Look at this photograph. This dragonfly's body is a reddish color and it has really long wings." Turn to pages 6 and 7. "And look at this photograph. It is a zoomed-in photograph. Is it giving you some ideas about what we might learn about in this part?" Have students fill in with some of their thoughts. You may reply, "Yes, it is a zoomed-in picture of the wings. We'll probably learn about the wings on this page." Quickly flip to pages 8 and 9 and then turn to pages 10 and 11. "Oh! What will we learn about dragonflies in this part?" Listen in to students' responses and coach them to say more about what they see in the photograph.

Image © Gerald D. Tang

What Are Dragonflies?

Dragonflies are long, colorful insects with large wings.

You may go on to say, "Let's read this book to learn more cool and interesting things about dragonflies. Give me a thumbs up if you are really excited to read this book. Me too!"

AS YOU READ

Read the text with expression and an animated voice. Use gestures and act out as you are reading to emphasize important parts and build meaning.

As you are reading, be sure to read and gesture in ways that emphasize important parts and support the meaning of the text. For example, you might hold out your finger and then your entire hand as you read page 8 or exaggerate your hand zipping through the air as you read page 14. You might read with a "wow" voice when you read surprising parts. Don't forget to linger on the photographs and study them closely because they support meaning and help with determining importance. After all, the strategies you use across the read-aloud implicitly teach kids to do the same in their own books.

Page 6: Pause after reading the heading to think aloud about the information you might learn from this part.

Model using the various text features included in the text, and prompt children to use their fingers to collect the things they are learning as you read aloud. Say, "I'm going to read the heading." After reading the heading quickly say, "Let's think about what this section is going to teach us. Do you have some ideas? I am thinking that we might learn about their wings and other body parts. A lot of animal books teach us about what animals look like. Were you thinking that too?" Then prompt students to use their fingers to collect the details they are learning from this section.

Pages 10–13: Pause before reading the text to study the photographs. To support envisioning, prompt children to act out as you are reading aloud this page and the following page.

"Hmm, . . . Let's study this photo really closely. As I am reading, will you act out with your body the information you are learning?" Turn to pages 12 and 13 and prompt the children to repeat the same process. Pause after reading page 12 and say, "Wow! We have learned so many things about dragonflies and what they look like."

Page 14: Pause after reading the heading to think aloud about the information you might learn from this part.

Point to the heading and say, "This is a new part. I'm going to read the heading." After reading the heading say, "Let's think about what *this* section is going to teach us. Do you have some ideas?" Gesture to the "Readers TALK about Books" chart and say, "Turn and tell your partner what you are thinking we might learn about in this part." You might voice over some of the things you heard children talking about. Again, prompt students to use their fingers to collect the things they are learning as you read aloud this next part.

Another option for shortening the read-aloud on this day is to read to the end of the book after reading the heading and thinking aloud on page 14, skipping the option to discuss unfamiliar vocabulary on page 16.

> SESSION 1: AS YOU READ
>
> **p. 6: Read the heading and think aloud about the information you might learn from this part.**
>
> "I'm going to read the heading. Let's think about what this section is going to teach us. I'm thinking we might learn _____."

Page 16: Pause before reading the text to study the photographs. Urge the children to act out as you are reading aloud. After reading this page, discuss unfamiliar vocabulary.

"Hmm, . . . Let's study this photo really closely. As I am reading this part, act out with your body what you are learning about." After you read this page pause and say, "Hmm, . . . Swoop. Let's stop to think about what this word means. Say the word *swoop*. Can you show me with your hand what it looks like when a dragonfly *swoops* through the air?" Then you might say, "Now explain what *swoop* means. Use lots of words to talk it out. What's it like? What's it not like?" Listen in to coach students to articulate the word's meaning. Then, call children back to explain the word. "When something *swoops* through the air, it is like it is diving down really, really fast. Show me again, with your hand, what *swoop* looks like."

Read to the end of the book.

AFTER YOU READ

Remind kids that readers have work to do after they finish reading. It is important for readers to take time to think about what they learned and talk about their books.

"This is such a cool book. It reminds me of some of the other books we have read about other animals and insects. Thumbs up if you loved this book and the photographs that Margaret Hall included. Yeah, she really taught us a lot! Let's think about all the things we learned about in this book!" You might engage in a whole-class conversation about some of the ideas or questions children have about this topic, or stay closer to the text, having children use the photographs and act out the things they learned about dragonflies in each part of the book.

Have children use the information they heard read aloud and the photographs to retell the key details from the first part of the text.

"Let's turn back to the first part of this book and use the photographs to help us remember what we learned about dragonflies and how they look." Flip back to the beginning and prompt children to look at the pictures across pages 4 to 13. Then, prompt kids to retell the details they learned. "Turn and teach your partner what you learned in this part. Remember that you can act out with your body as you are teaching your partner."

Listen in to students as they retell before reconvening to name back key details.

"I heard you teaching your partner so much about what dragonflies look like. You were teaching about their four wings that help them fly through the air and how dragonflies come in lots of different sizes. Some of them are really tiny, and some can be as big as one of your hands. I also heard (and saw) you teaching about their big eyes that help them see bugs and how their strong mouths help them eat the bugs right up. Munch! Crunch!"

Have children use the information they heard read aloud and the photographs to retell the keys details from the second part of the text.

Coach students to practice their retelling on the second part of the book. "Let's look through the pictures in the second part of the book to get ready to turn and teach everything we learned about what dragonflies do." Look through the pictures on pages 14 to 21 before asking partnerships to turn and teach.

SESSION 2

BEFORE YOU READ

Set students up to listen with a new lens as you reread.

Since this second reading may take place a few days or weeks after the initial reading of the text, take a moment to remind kids about the gist of this informational text. You might turn to the table of contents after reading the title and glancing at the front cover and say, "Readers, remember how Margaret Hall used photographs and words to teach us a lot of cool things about dragonflies—like what they look like and some of the things they do. Give me a thumbs up if you remember some of the things you learned from this book. Since we all loved this book so much, I thought we should read it again. Let's work together to learn even more from this book. Remember that you can act out with your body as I am reading, and maybe we will even come up with some questions and ideas about dragonflies as we read." Since this is a rereading, plan to give the students more responsibility for recalling the key details from the text. If you have read other books around this topic or content, you could also set the children up to be ready to talk across both books at the end of today's read-aloud.

AS YOU READ

Reread the text with an animated voice, pausing to study the photographs a bit more closely, and urging the children to act out with their body as you are reading aloud.

During today's reading, you'll want to think aloud as you come up with new questions or ideas. This reinforces one purpose for rereading. Plan for places where you will provide children with opportunities to practice this as well.

Page 13: Stop to demonstrate how you add your own ideas and questions after reading a part of a text.

"Let's reread these last few pages and see if we have any new ideas or questions about dragonflies." Reread pages 10 to 13, then pause and say, "I think their eyes and mouths are really important. They really help them catch and eat their food. I'm wondering what kinds of bugs they eat and if there are any bugs they don't eat. Were you wondering anything?" Urge kids to add their own questions about the details in the text.

Dragonflies have
strong mouths.
They crunch
and chew bugs.

mouth

12

13

Page 17: Stop to prompt children to add their own ideas and questions after reading a part of a text.

"Let's reread these last few pages and see if you have any new ideas or questions about dragonflies." Reread pages 14 to 17, then pause and say, "Are you thinking or wondering anything? Do you have ideas about what the dragonfly might do next—and how the dragonfly might do it?" After giving the children a moment to think, prompt them to turn and talk with their partners.

Page 20: Before reading the text, pause to study the photographs. Urge the children to act out as you are reading aloud. After reading this page, have the children discuss unfamiliar vocabulary.

"Hmm, . . . Let's study this photo really closely. As I am reading this part, act out with your body what you are learning about." After you read this page pause and say, "Hmm, . . . Hatch. Let's stop to think about what this word means. Say the word *hatch*. Can you show me with your hands what it looks like when eggs *hatch* from eggs? Turn and teach your partner about this new word—*hatch*." After the children turn and teach, you might recap some of the things you heard in a way that lifts the level of the responses.

Read to the end of the book.

AFTER YOU READ

Show children another book they are familiar with on this topic and engage in a whole-class conversation in which you engage them in thinking across the two books.

Get out the book you read on butterflies (or any other insect) and say, "Now that we have two books that teach us about insects, let's talk together about some of the ideas and questions we have."

You could also say, "Now we have read two books that teach us about insects. This book taught us about butterflies, and this book taught us about dragonflies. Let's talk together about some of the things that are the same and some of the things that are different in these two books."

However you decide to prompt the children, remember the importance of referring to both texts and rereading parts as needed during the whole-class conversation.

If you haven't read another book related to this topic or content, you can engage the children in a whole-class conversation in which they share their ideas, new thinking, or questions.

"Now that we've read this book two times, let's talk together about some of the ideas and questions we have about dragonflies." Don't forget to refer to the text and reread the appropriate parts during the whole-class conversation.

SESSION 2: AFTER YOU READ

End: After rereading, engage the children in a whole-class conversation.

"Now that we've read this book two times, let's talk about some of the ideas and questions we have about _____."

Shared Reading
Fiction

Text Selections

> *My Bug Box*, by Pat Blanchard and Joanne Suhr; use a big book version if you have it

> A familiar song, poem, or chant, such as, "Hickory Dickory Dock"

In general you'll want to choose books that are slightly above the independent reading level of the majority of your students, which at this time of the year will most likely be in the level B–D range. You'll want to make sure that that there will be lots of reading work to do that students will soon encounter in their independent reading. This is a replicable structure that you can use with any text you choose.

We chose *My Bug Box* because it is an engaging story at an instructional level, based on the benchmark for this time of year. There is some repetition that readers can lean on when reading in unison. It also offers opportunities for children to encounter prepositional phrases, contractions, inflected endings, and more complex pictures—all common characteristics of books at level C and beyond. This may be new work for some readers, but it is work within their zone of proximal development, and through supported reading, they will eventually be able to read this book with a high level of accuracy and comprehension. Likely, it will become a class favorite, begging to be read again and again!

On this first day of shared reading, you'll introduce the book and any important concepts that might be unfamiliar to your children. Using the title and cover, you'll want to get ready to read by making predictions about what might happen in the story. You might then turn to the first few pages, look at the pictures, and talk about the words the children expect to see. After previewing just a bit of the book, you'll read it from cover to cover, pointing under the words and encouraging the children to read aloud with you. Along the way, you'll stop to solve a few covered words, encouraging students to search for information using all three cueing systems and to use their super powers. You will want to display charts from previous units to remind readers of previously taught strategies. You'll work to make meaning across the pages, reacting to what is happening and generally enjoying the story together. At the end of the book, you'll launch into conversation and engage in activities to support comprehension.

WARM UP: "Hickory Dickory Dock"

Quickly reread a familiar text (a poem, song, chant, or chart) to build confidence, excitement, and fluency.

To warm up for shared reading, chart or enlarge this nursery rhyme that is likely familiar to your readers and sing it together. This warm-up—and shared reading in general—is meant to cast a wide net. Keep the tone welcoming and upbeat, perhaps saying something like "Readers, let's warm up today with a song that I think you might know well already! It is very catchy, so if it is new for you, I think you'll get to know it by the second or third round! I'll point under the words. Join me in singing as soon as you are ready!"

> ### Hickory Dickory Dock
> Hickory Dickory Dock,
> the mouse ran up the clock.
> The clock struck one,
> the mouse ran down!
> Hickory Dickory Dock!

After reading it a few times this week, remember that you can make small copies of this text for the children to read during independent reading.

Hickory Dickory Dock,

the mouse ran up the clock.

The clock struck one,

the mouse ran down!

Hickory Dickory Dock!

BOOK INTRODUCTION AND FIRST READING: *My Bug Box*, by Pat Blanchard and Joanne Suhr

Give a book introduction to provide the gist of the story and build excitement.

As you place the big book on the easel (or the little book under the document camera), tell the children what the story is about by weaving in some words from the text in a very conversational way. You might say, "Readers, today we are going to read a new story called *My Bug Box*, by Pat Blanchard and Joanne Suhr. It's about a girl who found a lot of bugs to put in her bug box."

Then, turning a few pages in the book, you might continue, "Let's look at some of the different bugs she found!" Look at a few pages and name some of the bugs, but don't go too far! You'll want to allow your children the fun of discovering the ending after actually reading the pages.

I found a little beetle on a leaf one day.

I put it in my bug box, and that's where it stayed.

Before the shared reading session, you should have covered up three or four words or parts of words in the text. We covered twig, sand, and toad. You might remind children, "I bet you saw that I covered up some words in this book! Remember, we can use *all* of our super powers to figure them out!"

Set a purpose for reading, and make it alluring.

Turn back to the cover, and with a gleam in your eye, add, "At the end, she finds another animal to put in her bug box. Let's read to find out what happens!"

Read the book fluently. Invite children to read with you right from the start.

As you read, point crisply under words to support one-to-one correspondence for the readers who are still developing this skill and to help all readers to track words together. Though you are pointing word by word, make your voice sound smooth and expressive. By the second or third time the children read the repeated refrain, you'll be amazed at how their reading voices mirror yours. You might notice it and briefly comment on it as you read.

Along the way, stop to solve covered words as you meet them in the text.

On page 2, you might choose to cover *twig*, nudging children to use the picture and the syntax of the sentence to guess what the word could be. You might expect that kids will say *stick* or *log*. Then, you could reveal the first two letters of the word, prompting the children to get their mouths ready and look at the picture. "Activate sound power *and* picture power," you might encourage. After revealing the word, read it conventionally. "It is *twig!* Right, that's another word for stick. Let's reread the sentence and make sure it sounds right."

On page 4, you could leave the *s* available and cover the rest of the word *sand* to drive children to use sound power immediately.

You will want to make sure that you are giving opportunities for students to get their mouths ready with consonant blends and digraphs as well as initial consonants, because this will help strengthen their problem solving with text.

On page 8, if children are ready, you might consider covering the middle part of the word *toad*, which pushes children to just the initial and final consonant, along with the picture, to solve the word. This will also make the work you are doing multilevel. Some readers will just look at beginning letters of words, so you can provide activities that will encourage them to move their eyes toward the ends of words.

Make a prediction before reading the ending.

Before moving to the last page, ask the children, "Ooh, what do you think is going to happen? Turn and tell your partner. I'll listen in!"

AFTER YOU READ

Discuss what happened at the end of the book.

After reading the last sentence in the book, you might look again at the picture and gasp, "Oh my goodness, what happened to the bugs? Turn and tell your partner!" As they talk, listen in and respond conversationally to model how readers enjoy, react to, and talk about books, such as "Wow, I can't believe the frog did that! Oh, you thought that was going to happen? That frog must be really full after eating *all* the bugs!"

Support children as they retell the story.

Shared reading is a wonderful time to bolster the retelling work in your classroom. You might ask your children to retell the story to a partner right away, as you circulate, giving some language support. If your children need more scaffolding, you might also consider modeling a retell first, then asking children to try. You could practice the type of retelling started in Unit 2 and continued in this unit, where readers use the title, pattern, and ending: "We just read *My Bug Box*. It was about a girl who found lots of bugs and put them in her bug box. At the end, she put a toad in her bug box, and he ate all the bugs!"

On this day, you'll set *My Bug Box* on the easel (or under the document camera) once again and proclaim, "We *get* to reread *My Bug Box* again today! This time, it will be a little easier, because we figured out so many of the challenging words using our super powers. This time as we read the book, let's really check to make sure that we are reading the words correctly."

Today's focus is on monitoring. You'll be developing the habit that readers are always checking that their reading makes sense, sounds right, and looks right. These ideas correspond to three cueing systems that are sources of information for readers: meaning (using the picture as well as background knowledge), structure (using syntax), and visual (using the print to attend to the letters and their corresponding sounds as well as the spaces between words). Cross-checking refers to checking one source of information against the other.

While yesterday you emphasized word solving using super powers, today you'll highlight the idea that super powers also help when you need to fix up words you've tried to solve. You will demonstrate that readers *do* make mistakes, but the really important work is to then check their reading.

DAY TWO FOCUS

✔ Cross-check sources of information

✔ Use fix-up strategies

✔ Read with greater fluency and comprehension

WARM UP: "Hickory Dickory Dock"

Quickly reread "Hickory Dickory Dock," adding a new verse, and boost comprehension and engagement by adding gestures.

Sing "Hickory Dickory Dock" once again, and this time, invent some actions that go along with the song and support its meaning.

Hickory Dickory Dock

Hickory Dickory Dock,
the mouse ran up the clock.
The clock struck one,
the mouse ran down!
Hickory Dickory Dock!

Hickory Dickory Dock,
the bird looked at the clock.
the clock struck two,
away she flew!
Hickory Dickory Dock!

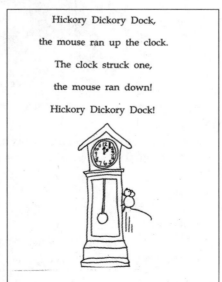

Hickory Dickory Dock,
the mouse ran up the clock.
The clock struck one,
the mouse ran down!
Hickory Dickory Dock!

Hickory Dickory Dock,
the bird looked at the clock.
The clock struck two
away she flew!
Hickory Dickory Dock!

You might bend one arm at the elbow and leave your palm open to represent a grandfather clock. Two fingers on your other hand can turn into a mouse running up your "clock," or invent your own gestures with your children! Convey how the clock *struck* with an action, to scaffold children's understanding that the clock is making a noise, probably scaring the mouse into scurrying down the clock! This supports children to think about what is *happening* in the song, even though it is familiar by now.

Today you might consider adding the second stanza to the song at the start of the warm-up and singing and acting out both verses. By the end of the week, you could add some picture support and create a book with each verse on a different page.

SECOND READING: *My Bug Box*

Remind readers to continue using all they know to solve words and to check that they are reading with accuracy.

Sometimes, you'll intentionally read words incorrectly and ask the children to check your reading. At other times, you may stop even when children read accurately, and prompt, "Are you right? How do you know?"

To do this work, you could leave words uncovered but highlighted, to signal to children that this is a "stop and check" point—a scaffolded way for everyone to practice checking.

For example, you might highlight *twig* on page 2 once again. After the children read it, you can stop and say, "Wait! Did that make sense? Check! Did it sound right? Check! Did it look right? Check! Okay, let's keep reading!"

I found a little cricket
on a twig one day.

I put it in my bug box,
and that's where it stayed.

As you read on, you'll repeat this process with three or four more words. Remember to balance reading correctly and miscuing. So you could, for instance, read the word *plant* for *leaf* on page 6 and stop to cross-check. "Hmm, . . . did that make sense and sound right? Let me reread it. Yes, I see a plant in the picture and it does sound right! Now, let's see if it looks right. No, if the word was *plant*, what would we expect to see at the beginning of the word? Turn and tell your partner, and then fix it up!"

You might also consider stopping and checking the prepositions *in*, *on*, and *near* on pages 4, 6, and 8, and perhaps *stayed*, which repeats throughout the book and gives an opportunity to think about tense. For children working on one-to-one correspondence, you might also model checking for spoken word to printed word matching. You might read more words than there are on the page. For example, on page 3, you might read as you point, "I put it in my bug box, and that's where it *always* stayed. Oops! There aren't enough words there! Let's reread and make sure our words match the number of words on this page!"

AFTER YOU READ

Link the shared reading work to independent reading.

Today, you can reread your "We Are Super Readers!" chart together. Ask children to talk with their partners about which super powers helped them fix up their reading when they checked and realized that something was not quite right. You might also continue the conversation by prompting them to discuss what they will do when they come to a tricky word in their own books.

DAY THREE: Word Study

On this day, you will focus on word study. Shared reading provides an opportunity to bring some of your word study work into context. You'll want to customize today's work to meet the needs of your readers. Look to your assessments—running records, letter-sound identification, high-frequency words, spelling inventory, conferring notes, and so on—to determine what will best serve your children. Work that tends to be relevant in these reading levels includes print concepts, hearing rhyme and syllables, matching consonant letters and sounds at the beginning and ending of words, segmenting and blending CVC words, and building a bank of high-frequency (snap) words. Keep this work lively and playful. Before long, you'll notice children replicating some of your word study methods as they read independently, assigning themselves lenses and goals for reading! Choose one or two items that your children need most, and then practice those skills in multiple places in the text.

WARM UP: "Hickory Dickory Dock"

Reread the song, adding a new verse.

Hickory Dickory Dock

Hickory Dickory Dock,
the mouse ran up the clock.
The clock struck one,
the mouse ran down!
Hickory Dickory Dock!

DAY THREE FOCUS

✔ Read high-frequency words in context

✔ Practice phonics work in context

✔ Develop vocabulary

Hickory Dickory Dock,

the mouse ran up the clock.

The clock struck one,

the mouse ran down!

Hickory Dickory Dock!

Hickory Dickory Dock,
the bird looked at the clock.
the clock struck two
away she flew!
Hickory Dickory Dock!

Hickory Dickory Dock,
The dog barked at the clock.
The clock struck three,
Fiddle-de-dee,
Hickory Dickory Dock!

Identify rhyming words to continue building phonological awareness.

Since the main shared reading text is not rhyming, the warm-up is a good place to emphasize rhyme. Singing songs that rhyme supports the development of phonological awareness. Sing "Hickory Dickory Dock"
once again, and listen for the words that rhyme. You might want to use Wikki Stix or highlighter tape to make note of these particular words. You could also ask children to name words that rhyme with some of the words in the song. For instance, you could say, "I'm thinking of a word that rhymes with *dock*. It is something that I wear on my foot," to nudge children to generate *sock*. You might choose a few other words and repeat this short game.

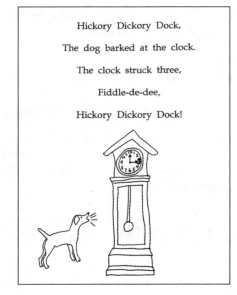

THIRD READING: *My Bug Box*

Choose a word study focus for your readers.

You might choose to concentrate on phonics work that will give kids mileage as readers, such as matching a letter with a sound at the beginning and ending of words. Perhaps you will do a hunt for beginning consonants, emphasizing the sounds when you find them. You could tell children, "Let's go on a hunt for the /b/ sound at the beginning of words. What letter will we expect to see at the beginning of words that start with that sound?" Alternatively, if your children are ready, you might hunt for ending consonant sounds, perhaps searching for /d/ in *My Bug Box*.

As the unit progresses, you'll want to be sure that your phonics work grows with it. Use your shared reading time to scaffold the increasingly demanding reading work, and as you use this template over the next few weeks, be extra thoughtful about focusing your word study on the needs of your readers. Know that the phonics work of this unit progresses from attention on initial consonant and initial consonant clusters to moving across words to the final consonant. Also, of course, base decisions on data. Plan to modify this template accordingly over this month of shared reading.

Some Possible Phonological and Phonics Topics for Study

◆ Producing rhyming words (e.g., *sand*, *hand*)

◆ Beginning consonant clusters (e.g., *cr*icket, *tw*ig)

◆ Segmenting and blending phonemes in CVC words (e.g., /b/ /u/ /g/ *bug*)

◆ Hearing and blending onset and rime (e.g., /b/ /ox/ *box*)

◆ Inflectional endings (e.g., look*ed*)

Search for familiar high-frequency words in context to support transfer.

Readers need to build their banks of known words. Shared reading is a prime time to spotlight high-frequency words. *My Bug Box* is brimming with high-frequency words that are likely to be on a kindergarten word wall at this time of year: *and*, *are*, *in*, *it*, *on*, *my*. In this text, the snap words are some of the words that change in the pattern, providing opportunities for readers to encounter prepositions, which will likely be new and challenging work for children reading these levels of texts. For example, page 2 says, "I found a little cricket *on a* twig one day." Page 4 says, "I found a little ant *in the* sand one day." Then, page 8 says, "I found a little toad *near the* door one day." These small words written in continuous text can be tricky for readers.

You might choose to search for particular snap words and highlight them in the text. Another method you can try is to give children snap words written on index cards, and as you read and meet the word in the text, children can hold up the corresponding card. This activity is simple to differentiate and tailor; you can use your data to determine the particular words that individual children do not yet own, and make sure that they hold cards with those words.

Study unfamiliar vocabulary, using context clues and dramatization to figure out the meaning.

Snug, on page 11, might be a new word for many of your children. Take this opportunity to add it to their vocabularies. After you read and bump into the word, spend time thinking more about it. "Readers, we've read this story a few times already, and we know this word is *snug*. Yesterday someone said that it rhymes with *bug*! Today, let's think about what this word means. Let's reread the sentence and then look closely at what is happening in this picture and the picture on the page before. Turn and tell your partner: what could *snug* mean?"

Listen in to the children's ideas, and then reconvene to tell them the meaning. "I heard someone say that *snug* is probably a good thing, because the page says, 'It was *nice* and snug.' And I heard someone else say that

It looked nice and snug.

because there were so many bugs in the box, and now the toad, there isn't very much room! *Snug* means cozy, or tight, as in tight space, not a lot of room."

Use the word in conversation to help it stick. Encourage children to use the word in their talk.

If you have a vocabulary word wall, *snug* might join the other words there. Because learners need repeated encounters with a word to truly learn its meaning, work hard to incorporate it into your language. Instead of discussing how full children's book baggies are, you might instead say "Wow, your books sure are snug in there!" or point out that the children's arms are "*snug* inside their winter coat sleeves" or describe the choice time cards as "*snug* in the pocket chart." Celebrate when you hear children use the word themselves. Push children to notice when a friend uses the new vocabulary word in their talk or writing.

AFTER YOU READ

Practice making snap words in isolation, before transferring back to reading the words in context.

After you reread the story, you could channel children to use magnetic letters to make any high-frequency words you practiced, before finding and rereading them once again in the book. Moving between word practice in isolation and in context helps to cement readers' knowledge of the words.

DAY FOUR: Fluency

On this day, you'll focus on fluency, supporting children to read accurately and smoothly with appropriate rate. It is by design that this is the fourth reading of this text, because your children will have greater word automaticity in this text at this point in time. This frees them up to work on pace and intonation, putting stress on certain words and phrases, and paying attention to punctuation to read with expression.

WARM UP: "Hickory Dickory Dock"

Nudge children to sing the song in their smoothest voices, with less teacher support.

You'll want the children's voices to outshine yours early on today. You might say, "We've been warming up with 'Hickory Dickory Dock' every day this week; you know it so well that you can sing it all on your own! See if you can scoop up all the words in each line as you read, like this," and demonstrate phrasing the words while sliding the pointer under one whole line of print. "Now you try! Your singing will sound so smooth!" Direct children to start at the beginning of the song and let your voice trail off, allowing only their voices to be heard.

DAY FOUR FOCUS

✔ Read fluently (with pacing, phrasing, and prosody)

✔ Spotlight different types of punctuation

✔ Deepen comprehension

FOURTH READING: *My Bug Box*

Reread the book in deliberate phrases and with stress on certain words to build fluency.

Many of your children will be moving toward the point in their reading lives when they are *beginning* to read with phrasing—or scooping up meaningful groups of words—on repeated readings, so shared reading is a wonderful, supportive time to practice. You'll want to model phrased reading, and the kids will match you! In *My Bug Box*, the authors use line breaks to signal the phrases, so as you read, be sure to group the words in the line together before your voice pauses, almost imperceptibly, when you get to the words on the next line.

To begin, you might say, "Readers, we've worked hard to figure out the words in this book. Now, let's really work hard on the way our reading sounds. We know these words well. Let's read like storytellers!" As you read, keep an appropriate pace, rather than slowing down or becoming staccato to mirror them.

As you are reading, you can also place stress on certain words in the same way that you can work on phrasing: just do it and children will pick up on your cadence. In this book, there aren't necessarily visual cues that the authors use to suggest which words to stress, such as bold or italicized print, so you might decide to stress the same word on each page, which allows children to use the pattern to support fluency. For example, you could read, "I found a little *cricket* on a twig one day. I put it in my bug box, and *that's* where it stayed. I found a little *ant* in the sand one day. I put it in my bug box, and *that's* where it stayed."

Pay attention to punctuation and the way it changes readers' voices. Make an inference about the character to bolster prosody.

On the last page of the book, you might point out that the character is asking a question. "Readers, look! This sentence ends with a question mark. Hmm, . . . let's look back. I think all the other sentences ended with periods. Oh, yes, they did. Well, the authors want us to read this last page differently. On this page, we have to make our voices sound like we are asking a question. But before we reread these words, let's look closely at the picture. How do you think she is feeling? How do you know? Turn and tell your partner."

Move among the children, listening in. Then you might reconvene the children and voice over, "I heard many of you say that the girl feels confused. Some of you noticed that she is touching her lip and her face looks worried because all her bugs are gone. So maybe she is asking a question because she is confused.

"Well, let's read this sentence, the one that ends with a question mark, with a really confused voice, and when we get to the question mark, we'll make sure our voices sound like we are really asking something. Ready?" and then once again, lead them with your own reading voice.

AFTER YOU READ

Boost envisioning by acting out the book.

You can bring the book to life by acting out its parts. Not only will dramatizing support comprehension and fluency, but it also makes shared reading even more fun and interactive! You could read a page or two and then have children make corresponding gestures. For instance, after reading pages 2 and 3, the children could mime carefully picking up a bug and moving it into an imaginary box. Or perhaps they could be the bug, first looking around out in the world and then looking around the bug box. Of course, pages 10–12 are ripe for acting out. You might ask some children to pretend to be the toad and some children to be the other bugs. How might they move? What might they be saying to one another? Engaging with the story together in this way also gives children ideas for what they can do with books that they read with their partners during partner reading.

DAY FIVE: Putting It All Together/Extending Comprehension

On this, the final day of shared reading with *My Bug Box*, you will support children in orchestrating all three cueing systems as they reread. You'll also think more deeply about the story together, perhaps engaging in a grand conversation about the new ideas the children have grown.

WARM UP: "Hickory Dickory Dock"

Perform the song to build confidence, excitement, and fluency.

On the final reading of your warm up, you might start by reviewing all the work students did in shared reading across the week, perhaps saying, "Readers, we've figured out tricky words and checked that our reading makes sense, used snap words to help as we read, paid attention to punctuation to make our reading sound like talking—whew! You've worked so hard this week!

"Let's put together everything we've worked on to make this our best warm-up yet. We'll make it like we are performing this song on a stage. We'll act out the words again, just like we did earlier in the week, but this time, because we've practiced so much, it will look and sound so much smoother!" If you added the third verse to the song, you'll need to quickly come up with some gestures to support the words. "Okay readers, stand in your spots and get ready to perform 'Hickory Dickory Dock'!"

✔ Orchestrate strategies used across the week

✔ Extend comprehension

FIFTH READING: *My Bug Box*

Let the children's voices overshadow yours as you read.

Begin reading with the children today, but let your voice trail off or even drop away completely. Notice it, proclaiming, "You are reading this challenging book all on your own, readers! Your reading has grown so much this week." You might add, "Rereading sure does help to make your reading stronger!" especially if you have children who need extra reminders to reread their own books during independent reading.

Consider inviting children who are almost, but not quite, secure with particular skills to lead the class in parts of the final reading. For example, you may ask a reader who is working on return sweep to use a pointer to direct the class to read across two lines of print. Perhaps you have a reader who is trying to activate sound power as he reads; he can teach the class about why the word is *cricket* instead of *grasshopper*. Shared reading is about role-playing your way into being the reader you are nearly ready to be. Use this time to nudge your children further along in their personal reading journey.

You might also decide to cover up different words than you chose on Day One. The children will most likely know all of the words in the story by now, but their work will be in naming the super powers they use to solve the covered word, and then confirming that the word makes sense, sounds right, and looks right. You could decide to take on a more pointed focus in choosing the words, like words with that begin with consonant clusters or final consonants.

AFTER READING

Have a book talk.

Push children to talk about the big thoughts and questions they have about this story, then grow those ideas bigger! You could ask children, "How might the girl feel when she realizes what happened to the bugs? What do you think she might be thinking here? What do you think about the toad eating all the bugs?"

Use shared writing to add to the text.

You could also decide to add some speech or thought bubbles to the text. For instance, on the last page, you might ask children, "What might the toad be thinking right now?" and then write something like "Yum yum!" on a Post-it and affix it to the page.

Broadly speaking, dialogue is a new feature in the books that many of your readers will be moving into. For this reason, you might also want to add quotation marks and a dialogue tag to the last page of the book, perhaps making it read, "'Now where are my bugs?' I said." You could also add another sentence that contains talking, such as "Oh no! The toad ate them!" You may end the session by asking the class to reread the last page of the book, inserting the new lines of dialogue.